EFFECTIVE

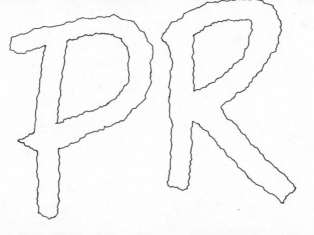

MANAGEMENT

A Guide to Corporate Survival

PAUL WINNER

SECONDEDITION

KOGAN
PAGE

To my wife, Mary, and to
Sonya and Daniel

First published in 1987
Revised edition 1990
This second edition published in 1993

Kogan Page Limited
120 Pentonville Road
London N1 9JN

British Library Cataloguing in Publication Data

A CIP record for this book is available from the British Library.

ISBN 0 7494 0997 5

Typeset by CG Graphics, Aylesbury, Bucks
Printed and bound in Great Britain by Biddles Ltd,
Guildford and Kings Lynn

Contents

Foreword

Corporations, like all other structures in human society, are founded and built on ideas. They can be made secure, languish or expand only if executive actions are guided by sensitive response to changes in the climate which surrounds them and of which they are a constituent part. That climate contains not simply market forces, lethal economic pressures during boom or slump, and trends that leave one type of product totally stranded while others swim off to temporary demand, but other factors, equally powerful, often unseen until they strangle the corporation. It is a key function for the PR cell of the corporation to keep the general climate under constant review to detect storms that are brewing and heading in the direction of the corporation's goods or services.

It is the complex and wide-ranging nature of that general climate that Paul Winner so clearly describes in this admirable book. Effective PR management depends centrally on awareness of the many elements forming the general climate and of the quarters in which turbulence is detected. Early warning systems of that kind are vital to the security of corporations or businesses, large or small. Size, in terms of market share, assets, available forward planning resources is no protection in itself. Until 1993 IBM or General Motors seemed impregnable world leaders. Their sudden plunge into massive losses seemed incomprehensible given the resources and experience at their disposal for protection and planning. Nor could their failure be blamed on economic recession alone. Part of their failure was caused by expansion and successes by their competitors who, it seemed, were more sensitive to the changing climate and more protective of their own flanks.

The lesson is plain; monoliths cannot survive in the ever changing climate unless they are able sensitively to predict its moods and shifts in their direction. The past record is no security in itself. Their size and past glory may indeed prove to be a weakness in a competitive jungle where predators are hunting for the larger animals who have lost their way.

The same principle of protection by awareness applies even more to the smaller corporation or business. By 1993 European small businesses went bankrupt in record numbers; thousands weekly mounting to millions monthly. It is true that many are victims of recession, throttled by mortgage fingers, fluctuating exchange rates, concomitant failing demand, yet it is equally true that others have survived precisely because their awareness of trends caused them to change direction in time to dodge the squall. PR management can be the effective navigator; this book is the navigator's chart.

It is tempting to believe that it concerns a modern problem brought about by undreamt of technologies producing undreamt of production in a new paradise of expanding societies of consumers. The ancient gateways to China are opening, around the rim of the Pacific Ocean countries are pushing their growth rates up towards 10 per cent while Europe's hover down on the low horizons of growth. That is the prospect for our times indeed and awareness of the trends becomes more complex, yet more rewarding for those who strike the correct course. But although the horizons have risen and widened for the next century and vast new markets are emerging among vast populations in Europe and the Pacific Rim, the perceptions among executives of corporations and businesses may not have increased in proportion. This book offers guidelines along which they may explore ways forward in the light of their individual contributions and experience. They will have goals made different by the character of their own goods or services, yet the principle governing the process, the imperative need to examine their performance in the light of new knowledge and technologies has remained the same throughout history. For me the classic illustration of the eternal principle was given by Ralph Waldo Emerson. He noted, in the last century, the great aqueducts which the early Romans had built with enormous effort across wide valleys to carry water across Italy. They were monuments to the ignorance at that time of the fact that water

rises to its own level making such physical construction unnec-
essary.

Our generation has constructed many equivalents of the
aqueduct – production lines based on obsolescent principles.
Newly discovered skills and capacities to alter genetic strains,
higher degrees of precision and magnification, revolutionary
new knowledge and corrective techniques concerning the
human body and the preservation of life, thus increasing world
population, are but a few among the fingers of change that are
once again reshaping our world as in past centuries it was
reshaped inevitably as discovery pointed the way. And we have
crossed a threshold of space that has already led major innova-
tors and producers to start physical planning for colonising
planets. The markets once locked behind the gates of flat earth
theory now move outwards to the stars.

This book is one small step that can help one sector of
action here on earth. I write to commend it, not as a business
man but as a retired international diplomat and Professor who
once taught international relations at several major universities. Why have I entered this field? There are two reasons. The
first is that the general climate and the PR remedies espoused
in Winner's book are one corner of the general climate that
embraces politics, economics,and cultural institutions. The
same principle governs them all – adapt to change or perish.
Arnold Toynbee described it as the sense of challenge and
response which is the woof and warp of history. Secondly, Paul
Winner is not only a respected and experienced practitioner of
PR but a man who has steeped himself in knowledge of the climate of growth towards international communication and
understanding. I came to meet him in 1955 when Professor
Gilbert Murray OM of Oxford, greatest Greek scholar of this
century and leader of intellectual and cultural thought in both
the League of Nations and the United Nations, wrote to me
saying that an outstanding student, Paul Winner, showed great
promise towards international understanding and needed
guidance. I saw him, gave it and have never regretted doing
that. He did not enter the diplomatic international field as I
did but after Oxford, inclinations led him into public relations
on the foundations of his desire to understand the ecology of
things that work together within a general climate. That is
what his book is about. I went on to be a senior Director of the

United Nations and aide to its Secretary-General Dag Hammarskjold. Our concepts join at a central point. It is one world. We must watch the weather changes in every quarter. They warn of storms and fair weather too . . .

George Ivan Smith
February 1993

Preface

It is today widely recognised that public relations (PR) has a crucial role to play in the total business system. The survival and effectiveness of any organisation are now seen to depend on the relationships it establishes with its 'publics'.

Understanding and managing the complexity of relationships which exist between today's increasingly open organisations is the basic function of public relations. While few would dispute this fact, not everybody is convinced of the ability of PR practitioners to perform this fundamental role.

It is the aim of this book to demonstrate the central role which the PR department or agency can and should play in the running of an efficient organisation, and to show how public relations is becoming an intrinsic part of every other management function.

Effective public relations depends in many ways on achieving the right balance: the balance between formality and flexibility in organisation structure; between encouraging innovation and relying on experience and precedent; between over-reacting and under-reacting to events. This book considers the choices to be made; it evaluates the relevance to PR of current management techniques and suggests appropriate ways of using the many good ideas contained in the literature of management theory. It also presents some original techniques for improving PR management.

Extensive interviews with decision makers in the PR departments of a number of industries, large corporations, local authorities and external agencies were an important part of the research for this book, and their views, which are quoted throughout the text, provide a valuable insight into various aspects in the practice of public relations.

The book should appeal to practitioners at various levels within PR organisations and to those wishing to enter the industry; it has been written with the requirements of the CAM syllabus in mind. It should also be of interest to those paying for the services of the PR practitioner and to those concerned with PR as part of the general management of an organisation.

In the 35 years in which I have practised PR there have been enormous changes. Since the revised edition of this book was published in 1990, the UK and the world PR industry have witnessed one of their worst recessions. Many of the established big names in the industry have merged or disappeared. But the role of PR has been recognised and accepted in every aspect of life and society.

1992 witnessed two significant and important developments highlighting the acceptance of PR and its relevance to the success and survival of the British institutions. The British Parliament and the Royal Family have both had to face 'crisis' PR situations which have made it clear that professional PR practitioners are accepted players in every aspect of such dramas as they unfold.

Paul Winner
December 1992

Acknowledgements

For the first edition, I should like to thank Penelope Silver of the London Business School for her help at the stages of interview design, field work and data analysis, and for her critical comments and suggestions on the various drafts of this manuscript.

Penelope Silver graduated in social sciences from the University of Essex in 1971. After two years as a consultant with Michael Spicer MP's firm Economic Models Ltd, she was for ten years on the faculty of the London Business School as senior research officer in organisational behaviour. She is now the founder and owner of Pi Consulting Group, an international multi-discipline management consultancy, and lives with her husband and family of boxers in West Sussex and France.

For this second edition I am indebted to the CAM (Communication, Advertising and Marketing Education Foundation Ltd), the IPR (Institute of Public Relations), and the PRCA (Public Relations Consultants Association) for their assistance.

I wish to thank my wife Mary, Sonya and Daniel for their patience during the agonising moments in the writing of this book and to Barbara Stevens, my invaluable PA, and to Donald Mackay.

Finally I am indebted to the organisations and practitioners whose comments are quoted and to all the past and present members of staff with whom I have worked in Public Relations for over thirty years.

Chapter 1

The Role of PR in the Total Business System

The central argument of this book is that public relations can and should play a many-sided role in organisational life. But the potential scope of public relations extends beyond the traditional functions of press relations and financial, corporate, industrial and technical communications. This has yet to be fully recognised. Increasingly, the public relations practitioner is involved in strategic planning, government, industrial relations and 'change management'. The role of PR is now accepted in every election campaign and in the running of the Royal Household.

It is proper and practical, as well as strategically sound, for the public relations function within an organisation to include the broad strategic positioning of an organisation within its total environment. Crisis management, social responsibility, community relations, and communication with all levels of government both within the United Kingdom and in international markets, particularly the EC, are all areas relevant to the public relations practitioner.

Progress in this ever-widening role for PR cannot be made until a reasonable working definition of public relations is established, covering its objectives and scope of operation. The confusing and even contradictory ideas which have existed make it very difficult for public relations people to practise effectively.

The following discussion of the problem of defining the public relations role is included not purely for its academic interest but in the hope that it will shed light on the best way forward.

WHAT IS PR?

The literature offers numerous definitions of public relations; indeed it seems that everyone who has had even a passing flirtation with public relations has been anxious to come up with the magic formula. But it is almost impossible to find two definitions which share common ground, and their value in practice is negligible.

The Institute of Public Relations (IPR) defines PR as 'the deliberate, planned and sustained effort to establish mutual understanding between the organisation and its publics'. It has been described as 'the engineering of consent', which presents us with an interesting concept but is not sufficiently specific to be practical. According to *Fortune* magazine, public relations is 'good performance, publicly appreciated because adequately communicated'. But this covers only one aspect of the public relations function; it ignores the role of public relations in explaining the reasons for poor performance, and of course it excludes from consideration a wide range of situations which have nothing to do with performance as such, whether good, bad or indifferent.

Public relations has elsewhere been described as 'the management function which gives the same organised and careful attention to the aspect of goodwill as it gives to any other major asset of the business'. But this definition assumes a closed system model of the organisation, and does not consider the role of public relations between organisations – which is increasingly important. More ambitious is the view that public relations 'is a combination of philosophy, sociology, economics, language, psychology, journalism and communication in a system of human understanding'. This may be true, but it does not provide the public relations practitioner with a very useful brief.

A common definition is so elusive because public relations is having to contend with important moral and ethical issues, as well as practical ones, on which opinions and attitudes vary enormously. At the moment these are dealt with on an ad hoc basis, but practitioners need to develop an intelligent appreciation of these issues and a coherent method of dealing with the problems which arise.

The relationship between PR and the media raises many

fundamental questions. It is very difficult to draw a distinction between objective editorial comment and public relations input, and between public relations and direct advertising. Opinions differ widely on what is or what should be the impact of public relations on 'factual' reporting. One industry PR director contrasted his own views with those of some of his colleagues:

> They would sometimes have different opinions about the role of the public press, and some very senior people think that the press ought to be helping industry to solve its problems and helping Britain. But I do not think that is what the newspapers are there for. The danger of that type of thing would be that you would be working towards a managed system of news, which I think is totally unhealthy and anti-democratic, and would demand misgiving. I think the press could spend more time talking about achievements and progress, but I do not think that is really a moral obligation. They exist to sell newspapers. I should like to see a more even balance of political opinions in the national press, but I can only live with the situation as it exists, and I cannot dictate the political attitudes of the Daily Express and the Daily Mail. . . .

An Institute of Journalists' conference was warned that:

> Journalists are increasingly misinformed by the government and others who attempt to manipulate the news. The Institute's President also said that journalists are being asked more often to suppress news because 'it would be in the public interest' to do so.

Bernard Ingham's own biography, written in 1992, highlighted the way the Thatcher regime managed the media.

PR IN ORGANISATIONAL LIFE

The role which public relations plays in organisational life, and particularly the importance attached to it in relation to other management activities, varies considerably. It can vary between industries; PR in the financial community is different from PR in the industrial field.

> It became ever more clear to me that PR as it applies to a bank or insurance company is very different from PR in industry or as it applies to a company producing a product which is going to be marketed and sold.

This view is common to the specialists in the different fields even though the basic function remains similar. The execution of the PR role also varies greatly, and evaluating its effectiveness is problematic because of the intangible factors involved.

The range of variation and the factors which cause it are discussed in later chapters. But there are points of agreement:

> I do not see PR as being a modern term that I would want to use at all quite frankly. I find that it nowhere near covers the sort of activities that I am responsible for. I consider my job to be improving the empathy between management and a large number of 'publics'.

The public relations director of one major industrial company, who is responsible for the board's external and internal information services and publicity throughout the country through press and broadcasting, advertising and lectures, estimates that at least half of his department's effort is directed at communications within the industry. This effort includes, for instance, generating a feeling of identity across the industry, and smoothing relocation problems. In terms of external relationships, he thinks that the real importance of PR

> . . . comes almost in a negative way. We have a tremendous potential for damaging the industry. In the case of a press officer, perhaps, taking a telephone call at home late at night, which they do, and perhaps giving a careless answer to a reporter . . . he could cause a strike . . . which would lose us thousands of pounds' worth of business.

Inaction can have as far reaching and damaging an effect as careless action.

> There is always a very strong school of thought about that, especially in the insurance industry, that tends to be a bit, maybe, introspective, and prefers to get on with its business and not be involved in this difficult thing of PR. People would like to be able to say 'Don't do anything, just adopt a low profile'. But we cannot do that all the time. We are too big, too important, have too many other influences on other people to adopt such a low profile. . . . The only result of doing that is that questions are unanswered in people's minds as to what we are really up to. But other people who are interested in us are going to make statements about us, so we have to do something about that. But there is always, I find, a fair body of opinion which says 'Well, perhaps you're

right, maybe we'll leave it this time round, tomorrow morning it'll go away . . . people will forget about it'. But in the meantime somebody's opinion may have been changed about what you are.

The target audience for public relations is determined by the activities of the organisation and any current problem areas. Public relations is often concerned with reaching opinion formers, that is the press, MPs, government officials and consumer groups. But in each specific situation the target audience will also comprise those groups in the environment with which the organisation deals; these are now increasingly described in the literature as the organisation's 'publics' (see Figure 1). It is a simple matter of identifying the relevant groups for any given organisation.

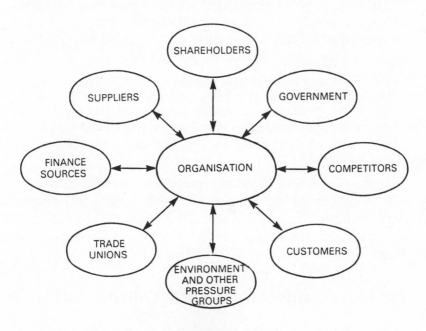

Figure 1
The environment of a business organisation

A PRACTICAL DEFINITION OF PR

PR is concerned with maintaining harmonious and understanding relationships between all the various parts of an organisation and all the groups which have a relationship with it. This could mean management, workers, shareholders, trade unions, suppliers, customers and government, as well as the public.

This definition of PR derives directly from developments in the area of organisation theory. Conflicting interests or competing goals exist within every organisation; eg workers' pursuance of their own best interests may be counter-productive and hence disruptive to those of management and the organisation overall. An open systems view of organisation recognises that there are many separate groups both within the organisation and outside it, all of which have vested interests. To a large degree it is the organisation's ability to cope with the inevitable conflicts of interest which determines its effectiveness.

The role of public relations is to try to resolve, or at least minimise, conflict through persuasion and influence; to avoid the need for forceful intervention such as strike action by a trade union or new legislation by government.

> I see it as a straightforward process of communication, of making people understand accurately and effectively the things that you want to make them understand, that you feel they should understand so that they are able to make decisions and reactions which in turn impinge upon whatever you want to do.

This is a very different kind of process from advertising, where one is concerned, not with maintaining a delicate balance between different groups, but with the simpler process of persuading one clearly defined group of people to behave in a particular way.

PR AND OTHER AREAS OF MANAGEMENT

The relationship between public relations and other management processes depends to a large extent on the particular organisation. In a sales-oriented company public relations is often allied to marketing and selling. News releases may really be a back up to advertising in trade and technical journals; effectiveness can be evaluated in terms of numbers of reader enquiries. When one is dealing with intangibles, with ideas, the link between public relations and marketing is less apparent and less easy to evaluate.

A lot of people today I understand are trying to marry marketing and PR, so the PR will be measured against the effectiveness of the marketing programme. So if, for example, a company will take various target audiences or target accounts and the PR department will use its techniques to establish a greater understanding and knowledge of the product, then it is now possible through that application of PR to give a bottom-line figure to it, if you like. In banking, that is not possible.

It is arguable that even in banking and insurance a bottom-line evaluation should be attempted!

There is one critical distinction between public relations and the allied functions of marketing, advertising and selling. Public relations essentially provides a service, not only to the organisation but also to individual departments on a needs basis.

I suppose the one thing which is different about public affairs from marketing is that however hard one works there are not all that number of areas where you make the final decision. There seem to be an awful lot of things where you are advising people to do things.

It may be a reflection of this weakness in the function of public relations that very often inadequate resources are deployed for getting information; staffing is often inadequate with no provision for extra (buffer) facilities to deal with unanticipated situations.

Although increasingly recognised as playing a critical role, the public relations function is typically under-financed. Many organisations spend millions of pounds on advertising, and below-the-line commercial activity, but very little on public relations. Taking all the organisations in the UK, not more than 10 per cent of their total advertising fund is spent on public relations. In terms of manpower, a very small percentage of time is spent on the PR function. For instance: a personnel director is often highly skilled in the personnel function – selection, analysis of qualities, salary reviews etc – but tends to have had very little training in communications.

But this situation has improved in the last few years as a consequence of two facts: public relations has broadened its scope, and it has also become recognised as an increasingly critical function. But the recession of the early 1990s has caused the process to be slowed down.

> I think it has changed a lot already, noticeably, in recent years, and I suspect it is probably going to change more. Again, change is often generated by what is going on outside.

During the 1960s, marketing was very much in vogue. Many marketing people rose through the ranks to head up their organisations. It is impossible to say whether having marketing people in key positions helped generate a climate sympathetic to the marketing concept, or whether, conversely, marketing was seen to be the newest panacea for all organisational ills (exponential growth was the solution to all problems) so that key posts were offered to marketing people. A similar process was observable when financial problems then became paramount and finance people moved in to head up large organisations.

	Category of Processual Relationship	Unit of Analysis	Level of Analysis
	processess internal to the organisation	individual group	micro-level
Organisation	processes which cross the organisational boundary	organisation	macro-level
Environment	processes external to the organisation	interorgan-isation	

Figure 2
The three basic categories of organisation processual relationships

The vogue problem in the 1980s was communications. But while there was a surprisingly high degree of consensus about the definition of the problem, the question remained whether or not public relations practitioners could and should assume the responsibility. Many ex-marketing people headed up public affairs functions. Is this because similar personality types are attracted to both public relations/public affairs and marketing, or is it a question of being sympathetic to market trends?

The (good) public relations person in the 1980s and early 1990s became accepted as the confidante of many chief executives, board chairmen, prime ministers and members of the Royal Family. The PR relationship is essentially empathic, interpretative and continuous. In the 1990s some PR practitioners and agencies performed a wholesaling function of bringing together and directing an ad hoc project team for specific assignments. This process continued in the recession of the 1990s.

In the 1980's there was a significant attempt to marry public relations with marketing. The argument has been between the purist and the generalist. The North American public relations scene, which the British tended to follow, moved on from the generalist approach and reverted to a purist public relations stance. But there are sound theoretical reasons why the generalist approach should be preferred. The PR marketing person who generalises has a better grasp of the corporate nature of their organisation; with broader perspectives they can make a more significant contribution.

It is increasingly important for organisations to function as openly as possible. Obtaining and accurately interpreting information about changes in the business, political, cultural and physical environment clearly necessitates effective two-way communication between the organisation and the external groups with which it deals. There must also be some control of the communication between those various groups, so that conflict is minimised. This is the role of public relations . . . or could be.

ORGANISATION SUPPORT

The effectiveness of public relations depends on a variety of factors which are examined in Chapter 2. However, in organisation terms, the support given to the function of the Chief

Executive is critical, particularly in the early stages before the personal credibility of the PR person has been established. Without the right person at the top, the most sophisticated function within the organisation is likely to be stunted. Another factor often critical to the success of the PR effort is whether or not the public relations practitioner is privy to relevant confidential information.

> We are lucky here because the Board do give it high standing. I go to all the Board Meetings, I am directly responsible to the Chairman. So we are not so much used as a fire service when something has gone wrong. If difficult things are coming up, most people . . . all levels of management . . . will remember to tip off the PRO. It is worth far more than if the man is taken by surprise.

> I attend all the Board Meetings. My predecessor's predecessor did not attend any of these meetings. The Chairman has been the instigator of this, and he has made it abundantly clear that he considers communications to be a vitally important task, and I cannot communicate and I cannot give the kind of service that he wants, unless I know exactly what is going on.

> And if the senior PR man is not involved at the senior executive level then probably the decision has been made that they wanted a dog to do the dog's job rather than to do a proper PR job.

Chapter 2

Organisation Structure

FORMALISATION/FLEXIBILITY

The key to all aspects of organisation structure is the extent to which roles are specified, and the range of legitimate discretion which the organisation allows the individual. The problem is how to fix the ratio between *formalisation* and *flexibility*.

In an organisation where roles are highly specified, where there is a high degree of formalisation, there is inevitably little flexibility, little opportunity for individual discretion. Conversely, where roles are relatively unstructured, and there is a low degree of formalisation, there is much more scope for individuals to use discretion, and consequently the organisation is much more flexible.

If we elaborate this distinction between formalisation and flexibility we can list a number of characteristics of each kind of organisation structure:

Highly structured roles		Unstructured
Limited discretion		High discretion
Inflexible		Flexible
Formalised		Informal
Easily disciplined		Hard to discipline
Hierarchy	v	Participation
Standardisation	v	Personal contribution
Specialisation	v	Common goals (generalist)
Equality	v	Recognition of merit

In public relations organisations (whether internal operations or external agencies), and in similar organisations such as

25

design consultancies and advertising agencies, it is crucial to identify and maintain the right balance between individual creativity and organisation responsibility; innovation and consistency in performance; inventiveness and cost effectiveness; autonomy and clearly defined roles.

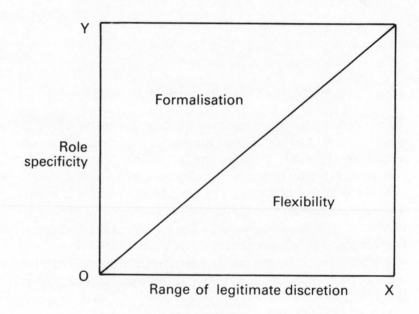

Figure 3
Organisation structure: formalisation/flexibility

DIMENSIONS OF ORGANISATION STRUCTURE

Organisation structure can be looked at in terms of the following three dimensions:

1. *Structuring of activities*
   The degree to which the behaviour of employees is defined, incorporating the degree of role specialisation in task allocation, the degree of standardisation of organisation routines, and the degree of formalisation of written procedures.

26

2. *Concentration of authority*

   The degree to which authority for decisions rests in controlling units outside the organisation and is centralised at the higher hierarchical levels within it.

3. *Line control of workflow*

   The degree to which self control is exercised by line personnel as against its exercise through impersonal procedures.

Looking again at the opposing characteristics of organisation structure listed above, any organisation which tends toward the lefthand side (ie is hierarchical, standardised, specialised and egalitarian) is described as a bureaucracy. Bureaucratic forms of organisation are also described in the literature of organisation theory as 'mechanistic'; non-bureaucratic organisations, in contrast, are described as organismic.

Mechanistic management system

This is characterised by:

1. The *specialised differentiation* of functional tasks into which the problems and tasks facing the concern as a whole are broken down.

2. The *abstract nature* of each individual task, which is pursued with techniques and purposes more or less distinct from those of the concern as a whole.

3. The reconciliation, for each level in the hierarchy, of these distinct performances by the *immediate superiors*.

4. The *precise definition* of rights and obligations and technical methods attached to each functional role.

5. The *translation of rights and obligations* and methods into the responsibilities of a functional position.

6. *Hierarchic structure* of control and communication.

7. A reinforcement of the hierarchic structure by the location of *knowledge* of actualities exclusively *at the top* of the hierarchy.

8. A tendency for *vertical interaction* between members, ie between superior and subordinate.

9. A tendency for operations and working behaviour to be *governed by superiors*.

27

10. *Insistence on loyalty* to the concern and obedience to superiors as a condition of membership.

11. A greater importance and prestige attaching to *internal* (local) than to general (cosmopolitan) knowledge, experience and skill.

Organismic management system

This, in contrast, is characterised by:

1. The *contributive nature* of special knowledge and experience to the common task of the concern.

2. The *realistic* nature of the individual task, which is seen as set by the total situation of the concern.

3. The adjustment and *continual redefinition* of individual tasks through interaction with others.

4. The *shedding of responsibility* as a limited field of rights, obligations and methods.(Problems may not be posted upwards, downwards or sideways.)

5. The *spread of commitment* to the concern beyond any technical definition.

6. A *network structure* of control, authority and communication.

7. Omniscience no longer imputed to the head of the concern; *knowledge* may be located anywhere in the network; this location becomes the centre of authority.

8. A *lateral* rather than a vertical direction of communication through the concern.

9. A content of communication which consists of *information and advice* rather than instructions and decisions.

10. *Commitment* to the concern's tasks and to the 'technological ethos' of material progress and expansion is more highly valued than loyalty.

11. Importance and prestige attach to *affiliations and expertise* valid in the industrial, technical and commercial milieux external to the firm.

A QUESTION OF BALANCE

It is now generally accepted that there is no such thing as the *best* organisation structure. One needs a balance between the two extremes of a *mechanistic* and an *organismic* organisation, but the correct balance for any given situation depends on a number of identifiable *contingencies*. That is to say, different organisation structures are best suited to different organisation tasks; the best organisation structure will depend upon the particular situation.

These factors derive from the formalisation/flexibility distinction illustrated in Figure 3 (on page 26)

1. *Size*
   Overall size has been shown in several surveys to be closely associated with type of organisation structure, especially in the size range 100–5000 employees. Organisation growth is associated with increasing complexity: the number of levels of management increases; problems of delegation and control increase; the number of separate specialist groups grows, so increasing the problems of coordination.

2. *Diversification*
   Diversification usually brings about a modification in organisation structure, typically through some form of divisionalisation.

3. *Environment*
   Environment conditions have important implications for the type of organisation structure which is the most effective. The key issue is the stability of the environment – how much uncertainty the organisation is facing.

   ITT provides an example: when faced with a climate of chronic uncertainty about the future of its telephone business in countries such as Chile, it built up a highly developed system of political intelligence to provide the necessary anticipatory and adaptive capacity.

4. *Technology*
   Technology is now seen more as a constraining than a determining factor in organisation structure. For

29

example, any effect the introduction of computers may have on centralisation is probably due to management's philosophy on centralising information and control than to the presence of the computer technology per se.

5. *Personnel*

The personnel in the organisation will affect the organisation structure, eg large numbers of staff specialists.

Three points should be borne in mind when considering these structural factors:

(a) Achievement of the organisation's objectives will be more likely if it adopts realistic policies, and its structure is designed to satisfy these policies. To illustrate: when a small sweets manufacturer decided to expand out of its traditional high quality market to produce a low price line for a chainstore, production could not be maintained at the new higher rate necessary for this contract because the company was still operating its previous (stringent) quality control policies.

(b) Factors of environment, size, technology and personnel vary between departments and divisions within an organisation.

(c) Structural factors are themselves interrelated, eg larger companies are generally the more diversified.

STRATEGIES FOR CONTROL

In a bureaucratic organisation, decision making authority is decentralised down to the holders of official roles. These are structured to take account of their specialised prescribed duties. A system of procedure and documentation is designed to limit areas of discretion, as well as to provide information on role performance.

Formalised procedures impose restraints. This encourages the development of a less centralised authority structure, and this in turn facilitates more flexible decision taking. So, as organisations regulate more and more behaviours, they decentralise. The reverse is also true: when organisations rely less on standard procedures for regulating and recording behaviour, other things being equal, they tend to centralise decision taking.

This gives two strategies for control:

(a) maintaining control directly by keeping decisions at high levels (hierarchic); or

(b) maintaining control indirectly by relying on procedures.

In a bureaucratic situation, both of these strategies of control may be used to try to achieve coordination between various groups of specialists with different goals. But both have their problems. With the direct use of *hierarchical control*, the higher up the decision is taken, the further away it is from the problem, and the greater the divergence between what was decided and what actually happens. With *control by procedure*, the danger is that the correct carrying out of systems may become more important than the coordination and control they were designed to facilitate, and worse, it may have a negative effect. For instance, it is generally accepted that too rigid adherence to budgets or purchasing procedures may reduce an organisation's capacity to adapt to change quickly enough.

Problems of bureaucracy

Three points need to be made here. First, several writers have suggested important negative consequences of bureaucratic organisation – although they have not disputed the contention that it is the most *efficient* form of organisation in terms of achieving the goals of the formal hierarchy. These consequences include:

- reduction in the number of personal relationships
- rigidity in the implementation of organisation rules
- increased use of categorisation as a decision making technique which decreases the search for alternatives (rigid behaviour)
- increased difficulty with clients of organisation
- increased use of trappings of authority
- by defining unacceptable behaviour, rules also define the minimum acceptable behaviour.

31

Second, problems develop where instead of *adapting* a bureaucratic structure, the system is just reinforced: for instance, by the setting up of committees overlaying the existing bureaucracy; the creation of 'super persons'; the creation of additional branches of the hierarchy; the creation of intermediaries. 'Nonpersons unperson persons.'

Third, all organisations have the weaknesses of their strengths; and the corollary of this is that all organisations have the strengths of their weaknesses, *if* they are prepared to accept those weaknesses. Strengths build into the weaknesses. If you ask an organisation what are its strengths, those are its weaknesses. The weakness of bureaucracy is therefore precisely its success. The significance of an organisation's weaknesses will be determined by the particular situation. The task of adapting in bureaucratic organisations is particularly important in a turbulent and rapidly changing environment.

THE APPLICATION OF ORGANISATION STRUCTURE PRINCIPLES TO PR

Most PR organisations belong to the organismic type because of the nature of their activity. The fact that growth tends to produce an increasing degree of bureaucracy explains why so many public relations operations remain relatively small.

The relationship between structure and process is a problem which continues to provoke much academic debate; this is fuelled by the difficulty of establishing any tests of the concepts involved. Organisation structure either facilitates or impedes organisation processes.

The problems of finding the best structure are common to all types of organisation, though the balance and the range of solutions varies between different situations and sets of circumstances. The best structure is determined by a number of sometimes unrelated factors.

Public relations organisations are particularly tricky in this respect because accurate evaluation of effective public relations is difficult. The reasons for this and the range of possible solutions are explored later. Where evaluation of the creative public relations input is a problem, so too is any attempt to define performance. And if performance cannot readily be defined, neither can it be easily controlled or monitored, and the whole process of planning becomes weakened.

From research, it has been possible to abstract generalisations about which kind of organisation structures seem to work most effectively in the public relations field. External public relations operations tend to be structured on the basis of client accounts, or grouping of client accounts. These are in effect the various groups in the environment with which the agency deals.

INTERNAL PR OPERATIONS

A typical structure divides into:

- Public relations office
- Press office
- Publications unit
- Film unit.

We have a Press Office which really comes under the operational side of the set-up. The Press Office deals with press releases, press enquiries and so on, and I think that works quite well because we have found that, over a period of time, we have been able to build up a relationship with the press, and therefore if something happens in the insurance industry we tend to get a telephone call from people in the press, to the chap in the Press Office whom they know, saying: 'What do you think about so and so?' or 'Can you give me any background?', or 'Would your company like to comment on this?' As a result I think we probably do get a bit more publicity than most other companies, actually.

There is a Press Office with about 10 people who deal with press enquiries and those press enquiries are in two categories. There is the selective and the enforced, and I try to get them to maintain a balance of selective and enforced. The enforced one is obviously where you pick up the telephone, answer a question, and the selective one is where you say 'Well, we are not getting over to this section of the media and that section and so forth.'

Publications units vary from a department of three people (as compared with the press unit in the same government organisation of only two people) responsible for 'the great mass of print and publicity that comes out, and which is translated into booklets, brochures, leaflets, stickers . . .' to the Publications Section of the Health and Safety Executive which 'is a key part of the structure. We have a bigger turnout of publications almost than any other department'.

The publicity part of internal public relations operations seems to vary considerably both in resources allocated to it and scope of responsibility. Typically it deals with direct mail advertising, conferences and exhibitions, and it will cover visual displays, lecture inputs and demonstrations. The Health and Safety Executive operated its own internal film unit, and produced about 21 films in total, all of those full-length films on either specific subjects and problems or broad health and safety philosophy.

In contrast, the public relations head of an American bank uses outside support services.

> Because of our limited, very small staff, I use an outside advertising agency, printers, design people who will help me put together a presentation. And because of my years in Fleet Street I know the people up there and, if I do not have time to write a speech or an article, I will call on a friendly journalist who will do something for me on a freelance basis. . . . So I can run what is a very complicated department with a variety of things because I have those outside services. They are not on contract, they are freelance people. . . . I use them occasionally because the requirement is so specialised that I could not do it without a lot of research, but also when it becomes impossible for me I cry out and I bring them in literally to assist me. But I do not use a full-time public relations consultancy. I do the work that they would do; I do that myself.

Internal communications is a key part of the internal PR operation's activities, and increasingly this is seen to be the case. In scope, this extends from the publications unit producing some kind of house journal, to an altogether more ambitious concept: 'We try to communicate with people in the terms which will be acceptable to them.'

> I suppose one of the most complicated areas, believe it or not, is dealing with our own staff. I believe that there is more misunderstanding between the management and its staff in a vast organisation – and I am not necessarily confining myself to my own industry here – than in almost any other field.

34

The following anecdote clearly illustrates the point. A bank manager in his late fifties said 'goodnight' as usual to his staff on Friday night, dropping his assistant off at the station a seven o'clock. He died of a heart attack in the early hours of Saturday morning. First thing on Monday morning the senior person responsible told the assistant that he would put up a notice to inform the staff of the manager's death. The incredulous assistant could manage no response other than to say 'You do it your way, but allow me to do it mine.'

The basic activities are fairly standard over a range of different internal public relations operations, and the organisation structures developed to carry out those activities are similar. Any variation tends to be in overall size, and resources – both manpower and finance. The sample ranged from a full-time staff of nearly 200 in the public relations function of one government department, to 40 in one of the clearing banks, 20 in local government, and less than 10 in several medium to large organisations, in both the private and public sectors. But the latest research in 1992 from *PR Week* indicates a growth of resources despite the recession in both public and large private-sector internal departments

Size seems to depend more on management attitude – being 'public relations conscious' is the phrase frequently used – than on industrial sector or size of company in terms of assets. One of the clearing banks has a public relations facility employing more than 40 people, an American bank has less than 10, and a large insurance company has a public relations head who is also in fact company secretary. All similar organisations, of similar size in operating and capitalisation terms, all in the same sector, but with very different emphases on public relations.

For internal public relations operations, regardless of size, the main operating problems seem to be:

1.   The range of different groups within the environment with which the public relations function must develop (satisfactory) relationships, and the problems of building these links in to the internal structure.

     Certainly in the financial public relations area we are talking about the groups that we have just men-

35

tioned, which is press, shareholders, stock market, investment analysts, and there is even a different range of audiences within the shareholders. Of course, because you have institutional shareholders like us and you have Aunt Bertha and so on, and you have to think about them all. . . . This is one of the great difficulties about trying to do effective PR, because the target audience is a bit diffuse, and . . . I think that the great difficulty that we all have is trying to talk to Aunt Bertha, who does not really understand very much about financial matters anyway, and how do you do that against the background where all the specialists are asking you for more and more information. It is not an easy one to resolve. . . . One of the things we try do in our annual report to help a bit is to have a sort of simplified financial statement at the front and then the more technical stuff for those that know their way around these things a bit later. But it is not easy because I think that the target audience is a very wide one.

The conflicting needs of various 'user' groups are one of the major considerations in the design of any information system, whether internal or external.

2. In terms of responsibility for public relations, there seems to be a certain delicacy between line management and the public relations function. One can appreciate the problems. First, public relations is both a conscious activity and, of course, part of the way in which every individual in the organisation behaves both to other people within that organisation and to the world at large. Second, public relations is essentially an advisory function and not seen to be a significant part of the decision making process per se. Public relations considerations influence the choice between possible decisions (government help to declining industries provide an obvious example). In this context, the importance of open support for the public relations function from the chief executive is obvious. The decision to close a large proportion of the UK's pits in October 1992 illustrates this dilemma. British Coal, the Department of Energy and the DTI, all failed to antici-

pate the reaction of MPs, constituents in the areas of the threatened pits, the media and the public at large. Did Michael Heseltine and the Prime Minister consult their PR advisers?

Some public relations heads feel a lack of support from other functions. Sometimes this extends to a disagreement among colleagues about how to handle potentially difficult situations vis à vis the press. The public relations head of an American bank occasionally finds it difficult to convince senior line management that an open, honest approach to the press is the best policy.

Some senior industry officials take the view that the role of the press is to help industry to print comment that is favourable to management, and in this view they differ from the industry's public relations chief who believes that above all the press must be free.

The conflict is sometimes exacerbated by the geographical distances between head office and branches.

> Not only do we have people at the headquarters, but also we have, at our other levels of management within the organisation, like at the regional headquarters and indeed in a lower level at the divisional level, people who are public relations or public affairs experts, who get functional guidance from me and who are part of the management of the local organisation they are located in. For example, with the ever-expanding use of local radio, I will give them functional guidance as to how we should deal with this phenomenon, and these people will carry out that function within the framework of the general management within the area.

> There are always conflicts where you can have a headquarters and regional levels underneath it, if you have within the regional levels financial accountability and general management control, because it means that functionally I cannot order the public relations people to do things, I have to advise and cajole and persuade them to do things. And in a way it slows up the process of management. But on the other hand, if I had immediate control over these people and could tell them to do things which they must do, then I could affect the financial structure of the region.

3. A basic problem in organising public relations is that its scope covers both on-going, continuous work and also

ad hoc tasks. These are like a series of continuous eruptions on the surface of the existing workload. 'Eruptions' rather than 'interruptions' – the term which management generally uses advisedly, since the public relations team cannot afford to be continually interrupted. So while the on-going tasks can to a certain extent be planned and controlled, there must be planning of a kind to cope with such contingencies

One solution is to bring in extra resources from outside on a temporary basis, as a kind of buffer. Another way to match the resources to the needs is to redeploy existing staff. For example, to co-opt people to act with ad hoc projects like exhibitions at a local level. Here the problem becomes one of delegation, and the perennial question is whether one delegates work or responsibility.

Finally, there are some very interesting developments in the role of public relations noted from the views which public relations chiefs hold about the growth and changes in their own operations. Most seem sure that a significant change comes from some kind of external impetus: a changed corporate objective, a general conditioning of society to expect higher standards of safety, the effects of corporate planning, or plans for privatisation.

EXTERNAL PR AGENCIES

The key problem for the organisation structure of external public relations agencies is to cope with on-going workloads and ad hoc tasks at the same time. The option available to internal operations of going outside is hardly so attractive to a competitive agency, and so the flexibility must be in-built. This is largely a question of 'role structuring' and maintaining good working relationships between various parts of the organisation. This range of possibilities of organisation design is discussed next.

Chapter 3

Role Problems: Conflict, Ambiguity and Stress

CHANGE MANAGEMENT – A NEW PR ROLE?

Organisations are no more and no less than composites of individual human personalities.

If all behaviour were totally random and completely unpredictable, any kind of social existence ('social' here means interacting with other people) would be extremely difficult if not intolerable for most of us. Fortunately, human behaviour does tend to exhibit certain standard patterns. Within any organisation, people occupying particular positions will be expected to behave in particular ways. Frequently positions carry clearly visible labels: eg mode of dress, style of office, calibre of car. Such labels provide clues to any individual's position within the organisation, and so help other people to select appropriate ways of behaving towards them. Consequently, each position becomes associated with a defined range of acceptable behaviours and these act to a greater or lesser degree as a constraint on the natural behaviour of the individual.

Considerable problems can emerge, both for the individual and the organisation as a whole, where there exists either conflict or ambiguity about the range of expected behaviours. The identification of such problems, and their resolution, is discussed below.

THE CONCEPT OF ROLE

Social systems – whether organisations, work groups or the family – are made up of a set of related social positions. Associated with every position in an organisation is a set of

39

activities and expected ways of behaving. These form the basis of the *role* to be performed for that position. A role is a set of expectations applied to the occupant of a position. In this way the concept of role links the individual personality into the organisation.

Associated with any given role is a set of expected behaviours. This expected standard of behaviour is essential in any social system, to introduce a level of certainty and stability into human relationships. An important part of the socialisation process involves developing an understanding of the responses of other individuals, so that these responses may be predicted and behaviour modified accordingly. If there were no stability or certainty about people's behaviour patterns, there could be no social interaction and hence no organisations. It is precisely because of the regularity of behaviour associated with specific roles that organisations and societies exist over and above the sum of the individuals within them.

A role can be visualised as the *context within which behaviour takes place*. This context is defined by the *structure and environment of the organisation*. But within the defined role, the behaviour of the role occupant will also be affected by many *variables*, eg his or her own personality, his or her response to other individuals, and indeed their response to his or her behaviour.

The crucial distinction is between the role and the role occupant; the role exists as something quite independent of the individual who currently happens to fill that role.

The concept of role, therefore, not only links the individual personality to the organisation, it also links the structural and dynamic processes of organisations.

RELATIONSHIPS INVOLVING TWO PEOPLE ONLY

The most simple form of relationship is a *two-way* interactive process (see Figure 4). Assuming a simple relationship between A and B, one could analyse:

(a) the structure of the two positions

(b) the conceptions A and B both have of their own role

(c)   the expectations A and B have of each other's role

(d)   the sanctions (reward and punishments) which each may use to ensure compliance from the other.

One of the most universally applicable examples of a two person relationship is, of course, the marriage partnership. Both spouses will have ideas not only about how they themselves want to behave, but also about how they want the other spouse to behave. More importantly, there is a wide range of options available to one spouse who seeks to change the behaviour of the other; that is, a wide range of sanctions which can be used to ensure the other's compliance.

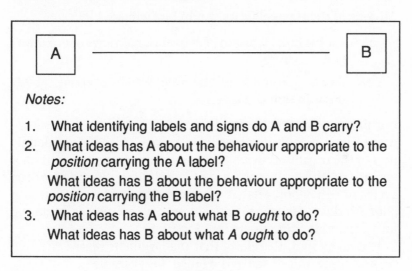

Figure 4
A simple model – the two-person relationship

ROLE ANALYSIS

The concept of role and the techniques of role analysis are helpful in understanding and interpreting the patterns of organisation and social behaviour. They enable the prediction of behaviour and hence help the individual to act accordingly.

The basic question for any public relations organisation is: what can be done to reduce the incidence of role conflict and ambiguity, and to make the effects of these conditions (when they cannot be avoided) the least damaging to the person and to the organisation? The range of possibilities to be considered is as follows:

1. Introduce direct structural changes into the organisation

2. Introduce new criteria of selection and placement.

3. Increase the tolerance and coping qualities of individuals.

4. Strengthen the personal bonds among members of the organisation.

All four of these possibilities would be facilitated by:

(a) a substantial revision of conventional views of organisation structure;

(b) direct utilisation of the role set in bringing about organisation change.

Formal organisation charts do not give a realistic representation of how organisations actually behave. A preferred definition of the organisation would be in terms of an open system, a system of roles. It consists of continuing, interdependent cycles of behaviour, related in terms of their contribution to a joint product. Hence, no role in an organisation is intact or fully separable from others (see Figure 5)

It is suggested, therefore, that management regard the role set as a basic unit of analysis. Hence, for example:

1. To change behaviour of an individual or the content of his or her role requires a complementary change in the expectations of others in his or her role set.

2. Plans to change behaviour should be directed at the natural group, not at the individual in isolation from his or her role set.

3. Changes should only be introduced if there is awareness of the implications for all members of the role set.

Figure 5
Three views of organisation structure

Assume that an issue has arisen involving the performance and task requirements for position C6, one of 16 jobs at the first level of supervision in the organisation:

1. Conventional organisation chart/approaches to management would regard this as an issue to be settled between the immediate supervisor and the subordinate whose job is at issue, viz B2 and C6.

2. The theory of overlapping group structures would see this issue as involving group two 'organisation families', primarily within the group consisting of supervisor B2 and subordinates C5, C6, C7 and C8; secondarily between c6 and his/her own subordinates, D21, D22, D23 and D24.

3. To approach the same problem in terms of the role set, we would begin by identifying the role set for position C6, ie to include those other people who have expectations of the behaviour of C6 and who communicate these expectations to C6.

   These expectations of role senders ought to be *taken into account* in any process of evaluating and seeking to change the behaviour of C6. This does not of course necessarily require the meeting of all members of this role set to discuss every *issue* involving C6.

   To illustrate: The activities of the person in role C6 will be affected not only by his/her expectations and those of his/her immediate boss, but also by the expectations of the person in position 1, the managing director. Particularly important for role C6 is the fact that the managing director too will have a direct relationship with his/her clients.

STRESS FROM ROLE CONFLICT AND AMBIGUITY

Contradictory role expectations for the focal person give rise to *role conflicts*. These conflicts generally have the following effects on the focal person: they intensify internal conflicts; they

43

increase tension associated with various aspects of the job; they reduce satisfaction with the job; and they decrease confidence in superiors and in the organisation as a whole.

The strain involved in such conflict situations leads to various 'coping' responses; for example, social and psychological withdrawal. This response is damaging not only to the relationship between the individuals concerned, but potentially to the organisation as well, since the typical response to the stressful situation is to reduce communication and collaboration with the role sender.

Role ambiguity exists when the information available to a person is less than is required for adequate performance of his or her role. It is useful to distinguish between two types of role ambiguity:

(a) task ambiguity: this results from lack of *definition* of the role its consequences are dissatisfaction with the job and feelings of futility.

(b) socio-emotional ambiguity: this is where ambiguity exists about the individual's *evaluation* by other people. This type of ambiguity causes increased tension in the individual, and undermines both their own self confidence and their trust in their colleagues.

Role ambiguity appears, from the research findings, to be a prevalent condition in modern organisations. It is fostered by the rapid pace of technological change and the complexities of modern organisations.

Some roles are necessarily more stressful than others. For example, people in innovative roles within bureaucratic organisations are subject to much pressure by other people in the organisation to maintain the status quo.

Similarly, people occupying boundary spanning roles (ie where the role set of the focal person extends to cover role senders both inside and outside the organisation) will often be subject to conflicting expectations; these expectations are often difficult to predict and to control, and people occupying roles at the boundary often have the additional problem of limited power resources at their disposal. Specifically, they are likely to be unclear about (a) their responsibilities, (b) where they fit into the organisation, (c) who they can legitimately influence, and (d) who has formal authority over them.

One point needs to be emphasised. We have discussed the negative effects of the stress which arises from both role ambiguity and role conflict, but this is not to imply that all ambiguity and conflict is necessarily counterproductive. On the contrary, a certain level of stress is healthy, both for the individual and for the organisation. It can promote creativity and innovativeness, both of which are vital to the public relations industry. The problem is to identify and maintain the optimum level of stress within the organisation, bearing in mind that individual personalities differ markedly in their ability to tolerate and benefit from stress.

CASE STUDY – CHANGE MANAGEMENT FOR A PR CONSULTANCY

Such a description of the theory behind role analysis is necessarily abstract, and so is best developed in the context of practical example. This organisation has been chosen from the research material because its central problem is common to a great many public relations concerns: survival through and coping with the critical transitional phase in company development from the initial, pioneering stage of entrepreneurial activity, to the later stages of specialisation and integration. This transitional phase marks the critical turning point in the career of the entrepreneur. At this point he or she must decide either to stand still (which strategy may in fact prove impossible) or to opt for the alternative path of continued development, which will require him or her to organise the company properly. Many of the lessons to be drawn from this case apply just as much to the effective structuring of roles within an in-house operation.

As Figure 6 clearly illustrates, recent changes within the Chairman/Chief Executive's role set had effectively altered the balance between the two constituent parts of this role. Of all his relationships, those with people outside the organisation had increased as a proportion of the total. The implication of this was that the structural balance would shift towards the role of Chairman, and away from the role of Chief Executive. The role had become even more of a boundary spanning one; according to the theoretical arguments outlined earlier, we should expect an increase in the level of ambiguity under such conditions.

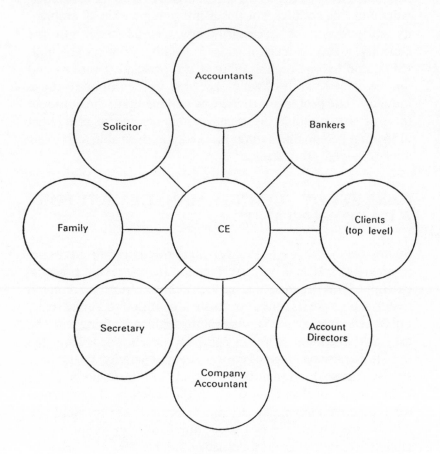

Figure 6
Case study: changing roles

(a) Current role of Chairman/Chief Executive

Previously all members of staff had related to the Chairman/Chief Executive on a one-to-one basis. This situation had since been improved by the channelling of relationships with Account Executives through the Account Director. Nevertheless, it is clear that the poor lateral communications within the company had developed precisely because of the previous direct lines of contact, from all staff to the Chairman/Chief Executive.

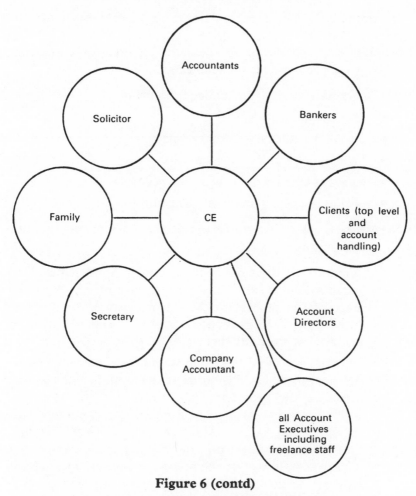

Figure 6 (contd)

(b) Previous role of Chairman/Chief Executive

Changes within the role set had provided a new *structure* for the role of the Chairman/Chief Executive. But the actual role can of course only develop if *behaviour* changes accordingly.

At this time, considerable ambiguity surrounded the development of this role. Basically, the ambiguity centred on the issue of whether the man at the top was simply Chairman or Chairman *and* Chief Executive of the company. It was felt that the metamorphosis from actively involved entrepreneur to Chairman was too drastic and hence not a viable proposition, and that the redefinition of the role as Chief Executive would be, certainly in the interim, a more intelligent acceptance of reality.

It was generally agreed that this redefined role would extend to cover such activities as the following:

- corporate strategy and policy formulation
- new business
- overall management of the company
- maintaining top level contact with clients
- acting as an advisory capacity on accounts
- overall budgeting and financial control.

Nevertheless, four discernible problem areas remained within this role definition:

1. Would other directors of the company be encouraged to pursue/develop new business opportunities? At what stage of the process would a new business venture be fitted into the organisation structure? And who would assume responsibility then?

2. What degree of participation would there be in top level decision making? The locus of ownership and control remained the proprietor; the power base for decision making was not split as in a public company and was therefore very strong. Moreover, it was clear that the unique position of the proprietor would continue to exert a decisive influence on the process of decision making, so long as the dual power bases of ownership and control were concentrated in this way.

Two points should be made here:

(a) The decision making process involves a number of different, overlapping stages. While a proprietor (or indeed a director of public relations) may typically insist on the right finally to decide to complete the decision making process by choosing among the available options, nevertheless there is much scope for involvement of other directors throughout the earlier stages in the process. And it is naive indeed to underestimate the influence of, for example, information inputs and reasoned arguments on that process.

(b)   Basically any organisation at this stage of its development must decide what sort of organisation structure
it wishes to take as its model. Specifically, whether to
remain essentially an entrepreneurial activity or
whether instead to become a typical professional management structure (see Figure 7). And of course the
basic principles underpinning that strategic choice
apply similarly to the development of an in-house
operation as much as to an external agency.

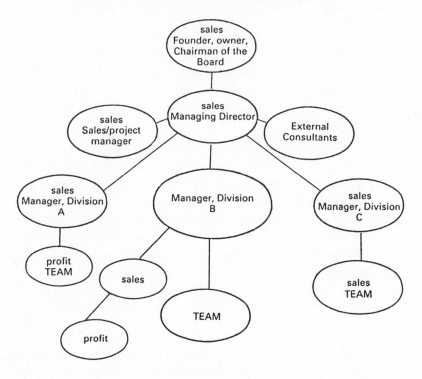

Note: Divisional split based on either functions or product/client/type of business

Figure 7
A typical 'professional management' structure

3.   Clients continued to expect the person to be au fait
with the day-to-day running of their particular account.
This caused problems when such expectations

49

conflicted those of account directors and executives (and indeed those of the top man himself) who would like to have seen increased delegation. One solution was for the Chairman/Chief Executive to be kept informed by his staff to a reasonable level of detail, but for it to be clearly understood that this communication was essentially one-way; ie it should not provide a basis for dialogue, still less dissension, between the Chairman/Chief Executive and the director or executive concerned.

A second strategy was to modify the expectations involved. Where the subordinate's expectations regarding greater delegation were congruent with the preferences of the Chief Executive, it was the clients' expectations which, so far as possible, should be modified.

4. Potentially serious problems could have resulted where the Chairman/Chief Executive made a commitment to a client, which a subordinate then had to implement. This could put the subordinate in an untenable position. The solution lay in some role negotiation between the two people involved, the success of which depended on the ability of each to modify the expectations and hence behaviour of the other.

One point above all to emphasise is the interdependence of roles and role behaviour. Any given role will influence and in its turn be determined by the behaviour of other significant individuals. Hence, for example, in this case study, successful development of the Chairman's role was dependent upon appropriate developments in the role of his No. 2, but those were, in turn, contingent upon the Chairman's learning to delegate responsibility. Equally, developing the effective role of the No. 2 required that changes be made in his relationship with co-directors, and indeed between those co-directors and the top man.

The key point for creative public relations operations is to establish a sufficiently tight control on creative output to be able to ensure that the quality of advice and implementation remains intact.

In many UK public relations operations the loss of top level control has led to a rapid turnover of staff and clients. They have had difficulty in structuring themselves so as to maintain high quality service to clients *and* loyalty among staff.

DIAGNOSING PROBLEMS BY ROLE ANALYSIS

It is especially true in public relations that any given attitude or action can have far-reaching repercussions throughout the organisation and beyond it. In the simple two-person relationship, A's behaviour is determined partly by B's expectations; so, to achieve any change in A's behaviour, it is essential that at the same time B's expectations also change. In the case study above, the Chief Executive could only distance himself successfully from the day-to-day running of client accounts if, at the same time, there was a complementary change in the degree of involvement clients expected from him. Furthermore, behaviour and relationships are constantly changing, and the dynamic aspects must be sensitively appreciated.

It is helpful to look at public relations organisations as a series of interrelated roles. The conventional organisation chart (see Figure 5) gives no clues to the informal workings of the organisation, ignores the consequences of each individual's behaviour on everybody else, and by taking a snapshot in time and projecting this forward, assumes a stability which is not realistic.

The exercise in role analysis set out in Appendix 3 is much more useful as a diagnostic tool. It effectively produces an *audit* of role relationships within the organisation, and as such can be used for both initial evaluation and subsequent review purposes. It identifies the potential problem areas.

The public relations management task is to remedy any problems and deficiencies which are identified. The critical theoretical point is that roles are interdependent. *Translated into practical terms, this means that any attempt to change roles and role behaviour must be a two-way negotiating process.* This applies of course both within the public relations organisation and in the work undertaken by public relations practitioners. It becomes particularly relevant in the communications audit work done increasingly by public relations practitioners.

THE PROCESS OF ROLE DEFINITION

The process of role definition, applied to the organisation discussed in the case study above, can be set out as follows:

1. Comprehensive listing of all tasks
2. Identify tasks which are:
   - clearly the chairman's role
   - clearly the managing director's role individually
   - potential areas of conflict
3. Discuss role definitions
4. Discuss conflict resolution together
5. Revise role definitions

To be effective, role definitions must be worked out participatively. They must also be flexible, adaptive and constantly under review. They must be explicitly defined and above all well communicated. It is therefore a necessary first step in the process for each person involved to be perfectly clear themselves on what they are prepared to negotiate over and what they are not. Following are a few initial suggestions for guiding the redefinitions:

Areas over which the Chairman maintains personal control

1. Overall budgeting and financial control
2. Distribution of profits
3. Allocation of resources among divisions
4. Corporate strategy and policy formulation
5. Structure and functioning of the Board
6. Vetting of new business opportunities/proposals
7. Top level contacts (social) with all clients
8. Direct contact with bankers, legal advisors etc
9. Direct contact with top decision makers in business, politics, the media
10. Acting in an advisory capacity (creative counselling)

11. Ultimate resolution of disputes between subordinates How far down the organisational hierarchy should this extend?

Role of the Managing Director

1. Responsible for overall profitability
2. Responsible for integration of various divisions so as to ensure coherent functioning and efficient resource allocation
3. Responsible for maintaining quality control, and providing Chairman with evaluative comments on the effectiveness of campaigns
4. Responsible for regular (three monthly?) staff appraisals to be discussed with (a) Chairman? (b) Chairman and person concerned? (c) person concerned only?
5. Responsible for staff development

Potential areas of conflict

1. Allocation of resources among divisions
2. Evaluation of divisional performance
3. Personnel policies
4. To what extent is/should the company be personified by the Chairman/founder?
5. Seeking out new business opportunities
6. Organisation within the company of new business ventures
7. Top level client contact: (a) to what extent should the Chairman be briefed about clients' accounts? (b) to what extent can/should the Chairman be able to commit the company?

Role of the Board and the Management Group

The definition of the roles of the Board and the Management Group must be made within the following parameters:

1. The Board has both legal and organisational responsibilities; the Management Group's responsibility is primarily to the company.

2. The roles of both the Board and the Management Group need to be precisely defined to remove ambiguity. But these groups should not be constituted in an excessively rigid or inflexible way, particularly since most people hold joint membership of both groups.

3. The (authority) relationships which need to be precisely defined are as follows:

    (a) the relationship between the Board and the Management Group

    (b) the relationship between the Board and the Chairman and Managing Director/principal shareholder

    (c) the relationship between the Management Group and the other members of the organisation.

Role of the Board

1. Responsible for long-term thinking and planning – ie corporate strategy

2. Responsible for setting overall company objectives and for evaluating/reviewing overall company performance matched against those objectives

    Objectives can be simple (eg that the company should aim for a certain level of total fee income, or for a certain return on investment) or they may be wider in scope (eg to include company philosophy toward personnel). Whatever the formal objectives, it is essential that (a) there is agrement among the directors over the objectives, and (b) these objectives are clearly communicated to all members of the organisation so as to achieve a feeling of real involvement at all levels in the organisation.

Role of the Management Group

1. More operational than the Board. Responsible for short term activity/planning – ie tactics, making operational

the corporate objectives defined by the Board

2.   Responsible for continuous monitoring of performance as matched against objectives

3.   Effective functioning requires good integration between constituent members, information sharing, high level of openness and trust, positive attitude toward problem solving

It is suggested that the best possible way to define the role and terms of reference of the Board and the Management Group is by agreement of those involved. A possible way to proceed is for all those involved independently to draft their own definitions, and for these then to be discussed in a meeting. Out of such discussions an agreed definition should emerge.

THE PR ROLES AS SEEN BY PRACTITIONERS

Difficult and easy relationships

Before analysing and seeking to explain the relative difficulties of working with various groups, it is obviously necessary to identify those groups. This in itself is often not the simple task it might seem to be.

It is hard to say which in terms of groups represent the toughest . . . I suppose the toughest thing is to define those groups.

First, there is the problem that particular target audiences may conceal great diversity. It may not be possible to find a common approach to communicating with this disparate audience sector. Second, although identification of the group may not be difficult, it may be hard to establish communication links.

You can develop channels of communication on the back of some obvious business link or common interest, but if the common interest does not appear to be there then you have to try and make bricks without straw.

So, for example,

. . . there is no immediate platform that I can think of for talking to the TUC as such. On an individual basis we think

55

there is some sort of platform like saying to the TUC General Secretary: You are an influential person. Why don't we talk? I think that is the problem – although we see the TUC or members of the unions as opinion formers there is not a natural platform for our industry to talk to the TUC. We are not unionised in this company; it might be slightly different if we were. So I do not think there is any natural platform. I would have thought that this is something a lot of companies have difficulty with.

So far as external relations are concerned, it seems that most difficulties will arise where there is no natural platform for dialogue, where no channels of communication exist.

Ironically, while some may assert that internal relations are the most straightforward to deal with ('because we are in control of what we say . . . you cannot control what is going to be in the *Financial Times* tomorrow, you can only do your best'), a more typical reaction reverses the problem.

I believe that there is some misunderstanding between management and its staff in a vast organisation – and I am not necessarily confining myself to my own industry – than in almost any other field. We are not going to be able to progress in industry in this country, I am absolutely certain, without a complete and through understanding of all the tensions and pressures and understandings which are necessary between us and our staff.

Internal communications are the biggest problem of all.

But the problem is more than simply a question of inadequate communications, and hence its resolution is much harder.

This lack of trust is not through lack of endeavour on our part, or lack of endeavour on their part, but they sometimes believe that we are doing things which are not in the best interests of the industry, and we believe that they are being done in the best interests of the industry. It is difficult sometimes to meet these different points of view.

This is of course an inherent dilemma. The best interests of the industry might not necessarily coincide with the best interests of the unions. Indeed, this is the rationale behind using the stakeholder model to analyse how organisations function: the various interest groups all have different objectives which may compete and even conflict.

We have to find ways of bridging that gap. I do not see this as an easy task, and those who think that it is an easy task, in my judgement, are deluding themselves.

And, in terms of the arguments presented in Chapter 1, this surely is precisely the increasingly critical role of public relations.

Role ambiguity

Regardless of specific activity, ambiguity about what one is doing or ought to be doing is as potent a source of anxiety and stress as work overload.

As far as workload is concerned, I do not have a problem. If I have stacks and stacks of things to do, fine, I just get on with it. I do not find that bothers me. But I do find that what you have described as the ambiguity of the situation or the lack of knowledge as to what is possibly required in some circumstances is a difficult one, yes.

Public relations is still an ambiguous function. The discussion in Chapter 1 illustrates this clearly. Whether such ambiguity is inherent in the very nature of public relations activity, or whether this is simply an historical observation at this stage in its development as a discipline, remains a matter for conjecture. What is clear is that PR practitioners, inside organisations and operating independently, have in hand a significant public relations exercise on their own behalf.

One feels uncertain what other people expect from PR. The parameters are very difficult to lay down. It is a largely subjective thing in many people's minds as to how you make up your mind whether you should be putting anything at all in this area. If so, how much so, what recipient should you choose for your favours? It is difficult.

Conflict

Perhaps surprisingly, it seems to be the ambiguity of the public relations function which gives rise to conflicts of opinion. Frequently such disagreements focus on the cost effectiveness of public relations activities (whether the ends justify the means, ie costs) rather than technical disagreement over the means themselves. Where there are conflicts over the actual carrying out of the public relations function, these tend to centre round the issue of when to react and when not to react. Opinions on this frequently derive from individuals' particular areas of responsibilities. They are functional rather than just attitudinal differences of opinion. Any solution must therefore seek to resolve a basic conflict of interests. For example: the public relations director of a nationwide organisation described his biggest problem area as his relationship with the organisation's 'legal people'. He believes very strongly in giving people the facts so that they may make up their own minds: 'It is a slow process of influence . . . very, very slow.' In contrast, the legal department prefers to disclose no information unless absolutely essential; to keep their arguments guarded until decisions are made, inquiries have reported, or legislation has been passed. Similarly, the public relations head of an international bank advocates 'speedy, honest, accurate' handling of any problem as soon as it emerges. Typically branch managers of the bank, or managing directors of subsidiaries, are reluctant to do this: 'I do not want to divulge that information at the moment because I will not be able to resolve that problem.'

Most public relations practitioners advocate a straightforward and efficient approach to dealing with problems as they arise; the basic philosophy being that to a attempt to conceal the truth is, in the end, very probably misguided strategy. The critical quality though seems to be the ability to judge accurately just when to react and when not to. 'I think, on balance, if you are in doubt you should not respond.' But this judgement can, of course, only be developed through experience.

Influence

Public relations is essentially seen as a support service, and so practitioners have to work through persuasion. 'The professional challenge is how effective your persuasion is.' To a large extent, the effectiveness of the PR person's attempts to influence will be determined by their own credibility.

One's credibility builds up over a period of time and once you have a track record behind you people will trust you and they will accept your judgement. Earlier on it is very, very difficult, and that is why you see, I think, PR people are in and out of jobs after a year or so, because they have come to a head-on collision. They have not had time to build up credibility before the crisis and then advice has been counter to what the management believes necessary, and out they go. Provided you have managed to build up that credibility and you have handled mini-crises effectively, even against the advice of management, you have done it in the way which you know is right, then when the big one comes they will stand back. I have already passed through that transition.

STRESS

There are many potential causes of individual stress within organisations. As we have seen, stress can be produced in situations where there is either ambiguity or conflict about what a person is meant to be doing and how they are or are not doing it. It is obvious that work overload can produce a high level of stress, but what is less generally appreciated is that work underload can become just as stressful for the individual. In fact, it is possible to identify the optimum workload, where the individual feels sufficiently enthusiastic and motivated to perform at their best. When the level of pressure increases markedly beyond this, it becomes a problem, and anxiety begins to diminish their performance. Equally, when the level of pressure is significantly reduced, the individual feels less need to perform well (or ultimately at all); their work suffers and they feel increasingly dissatisfied and finally alienated and depressed.

Obviously the optimum level of stress varies between people, and indeed, the same person may be able to tolerate different levels of stress over time.

This introduces another interesting dimension which is still being researched. Assume that Mr A has found that he performs best when he is under a certain amount of pressure – which we shall call level X. Suppose he has one major problem on his mind which is making him feel stressed. Will the effects of this be more serious, less serious or the same as if he were worrying about several, smaller problems? Cumulatively, would these equal the big problem?

This diversity of stress sources is one of the most significant characteristics of the public relations role. The PR person is in an invidious position. They stand between the organisation and the world outside. They are responsible to both for interpreting the other's perceptions. They have relatively little influence on shaping events but are often held responsible for many of the consequences of those events. Their programmed routine is constantly punctuated by series of crises – mini or otherwise. Most managers deplore what they call 'interruptions' in their day. The PR person does not have the word 'interruption' in their vocabulary; eruptions are the stuff of their job.

> To be a good PR man you have to be able to leave what you are doing and come back and almost pick it up at the full stop that you left it. It is an attitude of mind – a sort of grasshopper mind.

The public relations person is always in a stressful position, with continual pressure from a diversity of sources; and at the same time they have to cope with the extra pressure produced whenever one particularly critical issue erupts.

The public relations function is essentially a support service, an advisory function. The position of all staff specialists within an organisation makes them vulnerable to high levels of anxiety and stress. Research shows that they are becoming increasingly concerned about their credibility with line management. Public relations has a special problem in proving its effectiveness to a sceptical management.

THE RELATIONSHIP BETWEEN INDIVIDUAL AND ORGANISATION STRESS

A crisis has been defined in terms of individual stress levels among key executives reaching a peak, and so becoming an organisation phenomenon (see Chapter 7). Clearly there is a delicate balance between stress at the individual level and at the organisation level. The response of the public relations person is critical here, for to a large degree he or she is responsible for constraining the possible mushrooming of any stress which does exist within the organisation.

To illustrate: financial crises are frequently recognised inside companies up to twelve months prior to public announcement (twelve months being the period for disclosure of financial information). Clearly this is an attempt to stem the onset of a vicious circle of falling confidence. Similarly, abstracting from the individual to the organisation level, in situations of *underload* the organisation becomes complacent, unable to innovate or produce creative solutions.

COPING WITH STRESS

It is clear that stress at an optimum level is helpful for the effective working of both individuals and the organisation overall. Where the optimum level of stress on an individual is exceeded there is a real danger that the stress will mushroom and become an organisation problem. Stress can emanate from the very structure itself, as well as from the individual personality.

Where the source of the stress is structural, obviously structural solutions can be implemented. The range of possibilities for dealing with role ambiguity, role legitimation conflict and role activation conflict have already been considered in this chapter. Where the source is personal, people develop their own special ways of coping. The best advice is for people to try to analyse for themselves precisely what causes them to feel stressed, and to try some of the solutions advocated by others.

> There is self-imposed pressure, one is impatient. We all strive for perfection. I retreat, I have a cottage, I cut myself off from it. I am a devotee of the opera: once a week, inside Covent Garden, there is no world existing outside. It is a form of escape.

> Sometimes the very thing that gets you away from the doldrums of fretting about it is another problem.

> Now and again I have drinks in the evening with my Chairman or the Director General. We sit and chat. I find this satisfying in so far as it is uplifting. You think, I have got problems, but he has much more at the moment on his plate, and look how he is coping.

> Discussing things with civilised people is in itself an outlet.

> I do not get terrible gut-turning feeling in this job. Generally

speaking, I find the thing that most cuts me up is when I have major disagreements with my colleagues.

Stress is a very good word! The PR man is often in an untenable position, the demands of internal and external (in banking) are so opposing. He is trying to bring the two together, so he is the crossroads. That does create pressure and stress. You can cope by structuring the situation. If it is not possible to make a public statement – I have great faith in the leading financial, economic and political journalists – I often advise them of what is happening on an off-the-record basis, saying that they may hear some rumour of this event, I will tell them what it is now, but it is not to be divulged. So I keep lines of communication open on a private basis.

Chapter 4

Organisation Culture and the Individual in PR

The idea of 'role' links the individual person into the organisation in which he or she lives, works or plays.

Previous discussion has shown that the role of public relations as a management activity is frequently ambiguous. This applies whether we are talking about its objectives, its methods, its value and usefulness, or even its ethics. So any individual in public relations inevitably lives and works in an ambiguous context. There are, of course, both advantages and disadvantages in this. Ambiguity is for some people tantamount to freedom; other people find ambiguous situations very stressful. From the organisation's point of view, it is necessary to maintain the delicate balance between the minimum level of control and formalisation needed for the effective working of the organisation as a whole, and allowing individuals sufficient scope and flexibility to realise their full potential in terms of creativity and innovative thinking.

Organisations vary in the way in which they perceive and attempt to strike this balance. The two extremes have been described in Chapter 2. Bureaucratic organisations allow little flexibility to the individual; roles are explicitly defined; control, authority and communication are hierarchical. In contrast, organismic or non-bureaucratic organisations allow much more individual freedom; tasks and roles are continually updated and refined as the need arises; control, authority and communication are based on a network pattern of relationships.

These extremes can be developed, using additional dimensions, to give characterisations, if not caricatures, of organisations and the people living and working in them. The important point is that individuals have natural preferences for different types of organisation, which have been described as 'organisational cultures' (Handy). According to Handy, there are four possible cultures: the power culture, the role culture, the task culture and the person culture.

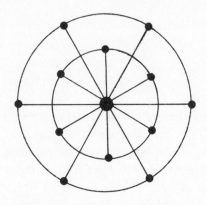

Figure 8
The Power Culture (Zeus, God of Gods)

Source: Handy (1976)

THE POWER CULTURE

A spider's web is used to illustrate power culture (see Figure 8). The locus of power and control is firmly held in the centre, which has direct connections to all functions and specialisms throughout the organisation. This is the opposite of bureaucracy. There are few rules and regulations, instead control is by personal authority

Usually, small entrepreneurial organisations have a power culture. As such, they can make decisions and react quickly and effectively in the face of change. This is why small businesses are often surprisingly adept at surviving under rapidly changing or turbulent conditions. Whether or not the responses made are the most appropriate ones depends entirely on the calibre of the person at the centre. Clearly, this is a potential source of weakness, and indeed many successful family firms plunge into decline when founding parents are succeeded by foundling children.

The other limitation is that the power culture's very structure imposes a constraint on growth. Increasing size must lead to decentralised decision making, control by rules and procedures, ie the antithesis of the power culture. The spider's web may collapse under the strain. Many entrepreneurial organisations in fact grow by spawning satellites. All have a high degree of autonomy, linked only in some financial relationship (eg a requirement to yield a specified return on investment) – Slater Walker, GEC and John Bentley's enterprises all operated on this principle.

Charles Handy caricatures his organisation cultures by referring to the gods of Greek mythology. The power culture is 'proud and strong' and calls to mind Zeus, 'the all-powerful head of the Gods of Ancient Greece who ruled by whim and impulse, by thunderbolt and shower of gold from Mount Olympus'. Such cultures are concerned with results rather than means and can be seen as ruthless. They provide the ideal setting for the competitive, ambitious and able person who is clearly determined to fight his or her way to the top, but middle management can feel very powerless, and a high turnover rate at this level is typical.

THE ROLE CULTURE

A role culture (see Figure 9) is basically a bureaucracy. Handy sees this as analogous with the clearly defined structure of a Greek temple, whose patron God is Apollo, the god of reason. The underlying principles of the role culture are logic and rationality. The strength of the 'Greek temple lies in its pillars, and its pillars are very strong: the different departments and specialisms. This kind of organisation is very effective under stable conditions but, as Handy has it, Greek temples are insecure when the ground shakes'. And indeed many large organisations with this kind of culture faced problems during the turbulent 1960s. There are inadequate links between the pillars, except at the level of the pediment – a narrow band of senior management – and successful integration is of course critical if the organisation is to adapt to cope with change.

Within a role culture, greater importance is often attached to the job description rather than to how the particular individ-

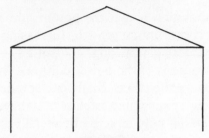

Figure 9
The Role Culture (Apollo, God of good order)

Source: Handy (1976)

ual fills it. Similarly, influence is through rules and procedures rather than any kind of personal authority. Fromm describes bureaucratic individuals and, clearly, whichever direction the causal chain (ie whether bureaucracies develop bureaucratic personalities or whether bureaucratic people select each other and stick together and operate organisations bureaucratically) only these kind of people are going to be effective and happy in such a culture. Role cultures are safe, secure, predictable and perhaps, too respectable. Bureaucratic life offers few surprises – good or bad.

THE TASK CULTURE

Most managers at middle and junior levels would, given the choice, prefer to work toward the performing of a task or project (see Figure 10). In small and medium-sized organisations, ad hoc working groups and project teams are established specifically to carry out a given task. This is often the case in well established, behaviourally aware organisations in fields such as advertising, public relations, design and management consulting. Such groups are set up for a clear reason, and can be abandoned or re-established as the need arises. Groups tend naturally toward entropy where the central task has been completed or otherwise disappeared, and cease to exist except in situations where they are kept almost unnaturally alive by fossilisation of their organisation. It is or should be clear to everyone working in a particular division that their responsibilities, loyalties and energies are directed toward achieving that division's task.

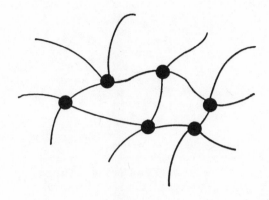

Figure 10
The Task Culture

Source: Handy (1976)

Handy comments that this culture has no totally appropriate 'presiding deity, perhaps because the Ancients were more interested in style and principle and power than in performance'. He sees the task culture as a *net*, with some strands thicker and stronger than others. Power and influence lie at the interstices of the net, at the knots, and derive from expertise rather than position or personality. Each work group operates with a high degree of autonomy, and since decision making can then be directed solely toward achieving the group's objective this type of culture is satisfactory from the point of view of both the organisation and the individual. Top management controls by allocating resources amongst the various groups, but it cannot exert more detailed day-to-day control over what actually goes on. It only has control over the output which, in terms of the ends/means distinction may well encourage innovation. But problems arise when resources are limited and groups must compete and politic for their share.

THE PERSON CULTURE

Person cultures (see Figure 11) are, in the pure form, unusual. The focus is the individual; and people will only develop some form of organisation, or subscribe to an already existing one, to the extent that it serves to further their own interests.

67

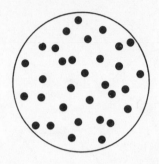

**Figure 11 The Person Culture
(Dionysus, God of Pleasure)**

Professional partnerships and of course many social groups, including families, are person cultures in this sense.

Structure in such cultures is minimal. Control is difficult since people like this will only accept whatever external control they choose to accept. Handy calls such structures Dionysian, after the god of the self-oriented individual and 'the first existentialist'. It is the perversity of such organisations that they do tend to develop their own momentum, and as soon as this happens of course the individuals reject their legitimacy.

It should be self-evident that most individuals who have opted to work in public relations would find a role culture incompatible with their personal preferences. Neither would such an organisation be very effective in this type of industry. Equally, a person culture is almost impossible to manage, and where there is direct and immediate feedback from a range of clients, as is the case in public relations, this is probably not a viable option.

Consequently most public relations firms begin as power cultures, where everyone is happy to start with, especially the power baron, but then middle-level executives become disillusioned and move off – often to start their own spider's web. If the company can, however, successfully manage to grow in size, it is most likely to develop a task culture, and as already pointed out, this is precisely how the bigger consultancies are organised.

Chapter 5

Performance

One of the most critical issues in the management of public relations is how to define and evaluate performance. Indeed, many would argue that this is the key problem area in public relations management, and that the special problems faced by PR people serve to distinguish this from many other types of management activity.

Evaluation is essential, not only so that comparisons can be made with other organisations, but also as part of the learning process which any organisation must go through to improve its understanding of the differences between desired and actual results.

The concept of performance needs to be clearly understood before any attempt can be made to develop measures with which to evaluate it. But satisfactory definition is very hard to come by. Most attempts at definition have been limited to consideration of performance in economic terms. This approach completely ignores all other facets of organisation performance: attitudes, perceptions, beliefs, motivations, habits and expectations of human beings.

Even if we accept this limited way of looking at performance, there remains a considerable problem in the selection of a satisfactory economic measure, which is applicable across different organisations and industrial sectors. Any chosen indicator of economic performance must be identified with some specific corporate goal. It will not be capable of taking into account, for instance, the different perspectives of shareholders and management towards the measurement of economic performance.

The very real problems surrounding the measurement of

performance have in fact been exacerbated by a failure first to formulate a precise definition.

SOME ATTEMPTS TO MEASURE PERFORMANCE

Using data from a cross-section of UK companies, Samuels and Smythe examined:

(a) the behaviour of profit rates and the variability of profit rates in relation to size of company;

(b) the relation between industrial concentration and variability of profit rates.

They presented the following conclusions:

1. Profit rates and firm size are inversely related.

2. There was a tendency for profit rates to fall over the period covered.

3. The time variability of profit rates and the group variability of profits are both inversely related to firm size.

4. Firms operating in highly concentrated industries have less variable profit rates than firms operating in less highly concentrated industries.

Samuels and Smythe measured company size on the basis of net assets, since this index is readily available from an analysis of company balance sheets. However, as they pointed out, this does not provide a totally satisfactory index, since (a) assets may not be properly valued, (b) some assets are valued on an historical cost basis, whereas other companies base asset values on replacement costs, (c) some companies are more capital intensive than others. Alternative measures of company size are turnover and employment. Samuels and Smythe chose not to use these indicators; as such information is not compulsory, its use would have reduced their sample size. It is interesting to note that in fact the various available measures of firm size correlate closely with each other.

The measure of profitability used by Samuels and Smythe was the ratio of profits (after depreciation but before taxation) to net assets. This is the 'book yield on investment' which, despite difficulties in its use, gives the best approximation to the profitability of a company. It has been suggested that there is in fact no other way of measuring return on investment for a continuing company.

In his study of company performance, Child collected financial data on the following:

(a)   *income*: ie gross trading profit less fees but before deducting depreciation; investment income added;

(b)   *assets*: fixed assets net of depreciation, with current assets added and current liabilities deducted;

(c)   *sales turnover*.

Child reiterates the remarks of Samuels and Smythe on the problems inherent in using net assets as a basis for comparisons across companies and industries. Hence, his main indicator of growth is restricted to a standardised score for sales growth.

The data presented in Child's paper do not indicate very strong relationships between company performance and the organisational variables studied. Child admits that this may reflect inadequacies in the measurement techniques used. More interestingly, he indicates the potential relevance of environmental factors for organisational performance. First, for example, there appear to be inter-industry differences in the relationship between size and performance, probably deriving from technological and market factors peculiar to different industries. Second, Child suggests that the concentration of ownership with control is not related to performance across the sample as a whole. Within the context of certain environments, the linking of interests of ownership and control may well affect survival and performance of the organisation.

It is precisely because organisations operate within environments which are peculiar to themselves that inter-company comparisons become so complex. Merrett and Lehr present an illuminating comparison of profitability between a sample of public and 'large' private companies, based on return on total assets (see Figure 12). Though they claim that this comparison is as accurate as is practically possible from published data, they make the point that no sensible comparison can be made between the performance of public and 'small' private companies 'since each is clearly specialising in areas in which they do not overlap. . . . They have different comparative advantages.'

	Weighted Average Return on Total Assets %	
Industry	*Private Companies*	*Public Companies*
Food	14.0	9.7
Drink	14.2	9.9
Chemicals	10.1	8.5
Metal manufacture	12.6	7.1
Non-electrical engineering	7.9	8.3
Electrical engineering	6.0	9.9
Other metal goods	13.1	10.5
Textiles	5.5	9.3
Clothing and footwear	10.2	9.3
Bricks, pottery and glass	10.8	10.5
Timber	9.5	8.5
Paper and printing	11.2	8.8
Other manufacturing	13.5	8.8
Construction	8.3	7.7
Transport	6.2	7.9

Source: Merrett and Lehr

Figure 12
Weighted mean return on total assets

PIMS profit models

A research project was undertaken by the Marketing Science Institute of Harvard Business School, into the on-going profit impact of marketing strategies (PIMS). The objective of this research was to provide top management, corporate planners, marketing executives and divisional management with insights and information on expected profit performance of different kinds of businesses under different competitive conditions. The research specifically aimed to answer the following questions which arise in the process of strategic planning:

1. What rate of return on investment (ROI) is normal in a given type of business, under given market and industry conditions?

2. What factors explain the differences in typical levels of ROI among various kinds of businesses?

3. How will ROI in a specific business be affected by a change in strategy employed? By a change in competitive activity?

The PIMS research team constructed an equation which explained more than 80 per cent of the variation in profitability among the 620 businesses subsequently incorporated into the PIMS data base. This profit level equation includes more that 60 terms composed of various combinations of the 37 basic factors (see Figure 13). Together with a second equation, which explains *changes* in ROI, this formed the basis of separate diagnostic reports which were constructed for each company in the data pool. For example: it was now possible to determine an average relationship between market share and profitability by comparing average levels of ROI for groups of businesses with different market shares.

The individual diagnostic reports gave an analysis of the ROI for each company, showing how this was affected by each of the 37 factors in the equation. The report could then be used as a standard of performance not only at company level, but also between operating divisions. The most valuable application of the profit model was facilitating an analysis of the reasons for past performance, and hence providing pointers for the best directions for strategic changes. Certainly the PIMS profit models provided a valuable contribution to the measurement, in economic terms, of company performance, as this is determined by environmental influences.

PERFORMANCE IN PR

It is clear from the above discussion that daunting problems surround the defining of performance, especially the selection and use of appropriate measures. Even taking economic performance alone, no consensus emerges.

Return on investment (ROI)
The ratio of net, pretax operating income to average investment. Operating income is what is available after deduction of allocated corporate overhead expenses but before deduction of any financial charges on assets employed. 'Investment' equals equity plus long-term debt or, equivalently, total assets employed minus current liabilities attributed to the business.

Market share
The ratio of dollar sales by a business, in a given time period, to total sales by all competitors in the same market. The 'market' includes all of the products or services, customer types and geographic areas that are directly related to the activities of the business. For example, it includes all products and services that are competitive with those sold by the business.

Product (service) quality
The quality of each participating company's offerings appraised in the following terms: What was the percentage of sales of products or services from each business in each year which were superior to those of competitors? What was the percentage of equivalent products? Inferior products?

Marketing expenditures
Total costs for sales force, advertising, sales promotion, marketing research and marketing administration. The figures do not include costs of physical distribution.

R and D expenditures
Total costs of product development and process improvements, including those costs incurred by corporate level units which can be directly attributed to the individual business.

Investment intensity
Ratio of total investment to sales.

Corporate diversity
An index which reflects (a) the number of different four-digit Standard Industrial Classification industries in which a corporation operates, (b) the percentage of total corporate employment in each industry, and (c) the degree of similarity or difference among the industries in which it participates.

Source: Schoeffler, Buzzell and Heany

Figure 13
ROI and key profit influences

More than any other aspect of management, public relations defies attempts to derive a below-the-line figure for any given activity. While the basic philosophy and rationale behind public relations are still so shrouded in confusion and ambiguity, attempts to define or measure its contribution are doomed. Is it the purpose of PR to create a situation where economic performance of the organisation is likely to be enhanced? Or is PR concerned with non-economic indicators: attitudes, perceptions, beliefs, motivations, habits, expectations? Is any concern with the latter seen merely as a strategic route to achieving the former, or are these things valued for themselves? If PR is concerned with economic facets of performance, must the search continue to try to find some way of giving a numerical, preferably financial, value to its contribution? If on the other hand PR is seen to be primarily concerned with the intervening variables – whether as a means to an economic end or as an end in itself – does it really matter that we cannot put a figure in below the line?

> I think that individual performance is that more difficult to evaluate than company performance. I do not think company performance is difficult. You can see the sort of impact you may be creating with the outside world, to some extent you can measure it – like people ringing you up and asking for your opinion, which presumably means you are worth listening to. That sort of thing is not too difficult. Certainly, on the back of advertising campaigns you can do a certain amount of measuring as to whether you are really getting through to people and whether your message is right.

Some PR practitioners stipulate that to be really effective, the ideas and concepts which they put forward must lead to changes in action. But of course this begs two questions. Firstly, it must be clear that either some positive action has been taken or, conversely, some action has been averted. Secondly, that action/lack of action must be clearly attributable to the PR activity aimed at achieving that result. Obviously activities such as exhibitions or sponsored functions allow for this kind of evaluation. Similarly, effective PR handling can avert some of the negative effects and repercussions of, for example, labour disputes, or other types of crisis situations.

As a general rule, it is probably true to say that the effective-

ness of PR is always difficult to demonstrate, and its cost difficult to justify, whether it is continuous or ad hoc.

> Sometimes senior management might consider that we go in
> for a few luxuries. . . . Some of our more earnest senior man-
> agement might raise an eyebrow, saying 'why do we spend
> so much time on things like that?' But it is all a coating on
> the pill. While they are reading about the beauty queen com-
> petition in the paper, they are also seeing stories about out-
> put and productivity, the results from various new machines,
> what we are doing in research – all this sort of thing is going
> in as well.

Such on-going activity may depend solely for its effectiveness
on a change in what are called the intervening variables of
organisation performance. Changed perceptions for example.

> We are now a profit making body who beat its contract by X
> million pounds. If you look in the Annual Report and
> Accounts we still get a contract worth something like Y mil-
> lion pounds from the Government to provide a service
> which is not profit making. So instead of being a company
> that loses Y million pounds, we are a company that beats the
> contract by X million pounds. That is a good enough proof,
> I would think, of the effectiveness of public affairs on the PR
> side.

But of course the effectiveness of any PR activity is heavily
dependent upon a series of extraneous events and circumstances. 'You cannot control what the *Financial Times* prints'.
Moreover, regardless of the merit of the PR effort, other news
events may overshadow its significance.

> You can measure to some extent, but very often we do a
> superb job, and the result may be nothing in the newspaper,
> because something else more newsworthy has happened on
> the same day. Or we might have done a superb job in killing
> a rumour or a story which has no foundation in fact. I think
> we can only get satisfaction by asking ourselves the question:
> Did you do that well? And you develop personal standards
> and self criticism.

> Senior management colleagues might sometimes be disappoint-
> ed because the results have not apparently justified the trouble
> they have taken, but when you explain to them that maybe
> something else of world importance has happened the same day
> or somebody else has made a similar announcement – as long as

you can satisfy them that they have done everything that they conceivably could have done – they are content.

The evaluation of performance at the individual level is probably similarly more feasible where one is dealing with an organisation that has built-in procedures for monitoring activities, costs, budgets and whether the agreed message is reaching the target at the right time. But it is also true that in ad hoc situations, rather than on-going routine PR activity, an agreed measurement formula can be found. People can be evaluated for their efficiency, cooperation, affability and positive approach. The real challenges are presented by crisis situations.

> Obviously I evaluate my staff on their success in reaching their objectives, as my boss will evaluate my success in achieving my objectives. But also on their responsiveness to crisis situations. That is a strong word, 'crisis', but to situations which are not planned for, and the willingness to work at something, not to panic, not to flap; to help, to guide – all those things. So one must never forget that in public relations the personal element is very, very important. It is the ability to always respond. So responsiveness comes into my definition of their evaluation. But it becomes a very subjective thing.

MEASURING MEDIA ACTIVITY

Measuring media relations activity is part of the growing trend towards evaluation of all areas of PR activity resulting from client demand for cost effectiveness and budget justification, and from PR departments and agencies seeking to win a larger slice of the marketing spend. This demand is being met by an increasing number of media evaluation services. The latest is Mediatrack, set up in 1992, which has joined Media Measurement, Media Works (a subsidiary of Romeike and Curtice) and EIT (which offers the Precis system) as well as CARMA.

The systems offer analysis of press coverage at varying levels of sophistication, but generally taking into account such parameters as a publication's circulation, the positioning of an article on a page and whether it contains the key messages that the company wants to see communicated. The slant of a story or the overall coverage in a particular title – concerning the company, brand or issue – over a period of time may also be part of the evaluation.

Some systems have taken the analysis of press clippings to new levels by producing 'bylines' reports – analyses of individual journalists' stances on any particular issue or company.

The bylines service breaks down every article written about the client, giving its type (news, editorial, feature or letter) and its degree of favourability, unfavourability or neutrality, and naming the published sources consulted by the journalist. These services also break down articles according to all the issues they deal with.

This information can then be presented graphically to show, for example, the favourable, unfavourable and neutral attitudes of individual journalists (see Figure 14). By matching attitudes against circulation, companies can assess how they are viewed by the journalists who are most important when it comes to influencing their target audiences.

The bylines report highlights individual journalists' interests and attitudes. They are a tactical, rather than a strategic tool. They will tell you who a journalist is talking to, what their history is, what their overall position on a company or an issue is, what they have written and how influential (by circulation) they are.

The media evaluation firms offer byline services to show their own cost effectiveness, since their charges can run into thousands of pounds. Analysing 1,000 clippings over a year can cost around £5,000, while analysing 3,000 clippings would be £10,000. But that is for the total service, of which bylines is only a part.

But there are cost savings from evaluation, too. A systematic analysis of media output allows a PR team to target journalists who are interested or informed about a particular subject, or whose view a company wants to change.

One health insurance company launched a care insurance package for the elderly. They used bylines to find out which journalists were writing about the elderly so they could be more specific in targeting them.

Despite its obvious potential for upgrading the media relations function, the demand for this type of evaluation is not great. Clients are not interested in journalists. They want competitive analysis or issue management or to assess the impact of last week's story. The UK has yet to catch up with the US in this respect. The US market is more about 'issues tracking'

WHAT THE PAPERS SAY ABOUT THE LONDON DOCKLANDS DEVELOPMENT CORPORATION

CARMA analysed 209 aticles about the LDDC published between January and May. The charts below represent a sample of its analysis. (LDDC is not a CARMA client.)

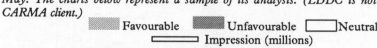

Favourable   Unfavourable   Neutral
Impression (millions)

Leading publications by volume & favourability

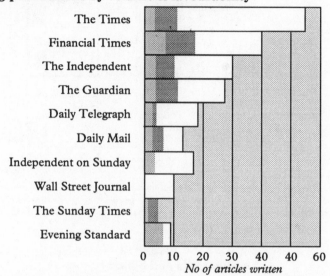

Ranks publication by the number of articles written on the LDDC and shows breakdown of favourable, negative and neutral coverage

Leading publications by impressions

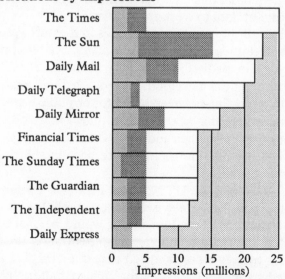

Ranks publications according to circulation multiplied by number of articles published about the LDDC. The chart also shows breakdown of favourable, negative and neutral coverage given to the LDDC.

79

Leading bylines by volume

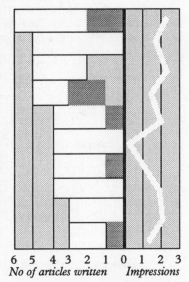

	6 5 4 3 2 1	0	1 2 3
Jason Nisse, The Independent			
Larry Black, The Independent			
Rebecca Smithers, The Guardian			
Vanessa Houlder, Financial Times			
Mathew Bond, The Times			
Neil Barsky, Wire Service			
Robert Preston, Financial Times			
Rodney Hobson, The Times			
Cathy Gunn, Today			
Alan Travis, The Guardian			

No of articles written   *Impressions*

Shows number of articles written, degree of favourability and impression made by circulation reach. So, Jason Nisse of the Independent has written the greatest number of articles and scores highest on the impression scale, but has produced no favourable comments.

Figure 14
Example of a byline report

Source: PR Week, October 1992 and CARMA.

and 'benchmarking' the competition. But in the US they use this kind of data to work the media.

While all the information used is in the public domain, journalists feel uneasy about the compilation of files on their work. Policing the media for objectivity – which might be construed as one potential development from bylines analysis – could lead to a meeting between an editor or publisher and a company chief where the latter requests that 'a more objective' writer is put on to cover their industry. On the other hand, such files could also make journalists more accountable for what they write.

For example, the US National Rifle Association was invited to take part in a televised debate with the Anti-Handgun Association, and was told that it would be chaired by a journalist who was both an expert and neutral on the subject. But when a bylines report showed that the journalist had a highly slanted stance on the issue, the chairman of the NRA went an hour early to the debate and quizzed the moderator on his qualifications for the debate. When confronted by the bylines report, the journalist was so taken aback and desperate to show neutrality that he went overboard to help the client during the debate.

The impact of bylines reports on media relations could clearly be substantial. They make media relations more targeted, more cost effective and more professional.

As media relations become more of a discipline in their own right, the mystique which once made them the domain of journalists-turned-PR consultants is being eroded.

The development of evaluation systems has in part been held up by a fear among some communications people that media evaluation is as much about testing their own effectiveness as it is assessing the coverage. Yet the opportunity the data gives PR officers to measure the impact of their media work will mean that vague acknowledgements from marketing directors that editorial coverage is a good thing do not need to go unchallenged.

Once editorial mentions are logged on a Media Monitor database, coverage can be analysed in a number of different ways.

- Information logged includes publication title and type, date, location, subject, type of coverage, messages (with a graded positive or negative weighting), prominence (size, pictures/graphics, position, colour and headlines) and likely source.

- The database can be cross-referenced to a media contacts database so that a value for each media title can be calculated. The value is based on factors such as readership/viewers, editorial quality and client or target audience perceptions of the title.

- These combined data can then be used to calculate a relative value for each media mention. The actual unit is unimportant as it is simply a way of comparing mentions.

Typical reports include an analysis of the appearance of corporate messages, looking at their frequency, spread and exactly which messages are used. Alternatively, the system can produce reports which analyse the coverage in a particular media

81

title or group titles, and location reports, which track coverage in a particular region or country.

Evaluating coverage by advertising equivalent – calculating what it would have cost to buy the same space – is useful for large consumer campaigns, both brand and generic. It gives a measure of the opportunities available and helps them to relate PR directly to their experience of advertising exposure.

The total media list before a campaign starts is split into three categories scored as:

- essential – 3

- important – 2

- basic – 1

Key words are agreed for every news release and feature contribution and these are given a numerical value. Points are also added for positive coverage or taken off for negative coverage.

Photographs are rated, too, along with the use of key words in headlines. Ten points in total are available for each press release.

The points for all items divided by the number of items is the measure of effectiveness.

- *Media reach* – the total audience reach of coverage that results directly from the PR campaign and delivers at least one of the agreed campaign messages.

- *Audience factor* – a rating agreed with the client for each of the target media, based on their penetration of the target audience.

- *Impact* – a rating for each item of coverage (again agreed with the client) in terms of its position, length, exclusivity and impact.

- *Message delivery* – most important of all, a score according to the number of agreed campaign messages delivered by each item of the coverage.

The system works like a spread sheet on a computer network. Cuttings and broadcast reports are analysed by the account teams and relevant information is entered on the system.

The result is a kind of at-a-glance summary of the coverage results for a particular period. The system also has a graphic capability but clients prefer tabular reports which they find easier to relate to the cuttings attached.

EVALUATING PR PERFORMANCE

An evaluation procedure to measure the performance of PR activity was developed for use within my own company, but subsequently I have found many of my clients and competitors enthusiastic.

I wanted to consider how to evaluate the effectiveness of client campaigns, bearing in mind the following criteria:

- time input

- deployment of total resources

- creative input

- communication between the client organisation and the appropriate environment.

Regular and accurate evaluation of on-going client relationships would provide invaluable information, which could be used as a basis to improve relationships, and to increase the probabilities of that particular business being renewed

It is advantageous when developing new business proposals, to be able to demonstrate to prospective clients that all relationships are regularly and systematically reviewed, and to explain the reasons for doing so. To facilitate a sophisticated evaluation procedure, three tools were developed:

(a) *checklist*, to evaluate objectively the effectiveness of client relationships;

(b) *questionnaire*, to elicit the client's subjective assessment of the relationship;

(c) *activity record*, to provide basic data for the objective evaluation, ie to be used as information input to the checklist.

83

Objective evaluation and review

There appear to be two aspects to the 'effectiveness' of any client relationship:

(a) from the point of view of the PR specialist/consultancy;

(b) from the point of view of the client.

Clearly the two aspects are closely related, but are not identical and hence should not be confused.

The PR specialist's criteria for 'effectiveness' are:

● no apparent indications of client dissatisfaction

● good prospects for renewal of the business

● profitability.

It may seem that client satisfaction would derive from an effective campaign, where effectiveness is objectively defined. To some extent this is so, but effectiveness from the client's point of view is substantially 'perceived' effectiveness.

The checklist in Appendix 3 was developed by taking a number of operational measures of effectiveness, and defining these as potential problem areas:

● time input

● costs

● clarity of role definition

● campaign effectiveness

● evaluation of creative input

● optimal deployment of resources

● implementation

● communication with the public

The basic formula for measuring effectiveness is: given the process of public relations activity, has the output been satisfactory vis-à-vis the input? Specialist departments and external consultancies alike need to be sensitive to all early indications of client dissatisfaction, and to react before that dissatisfaction can develop. The checklist in Appendix 3 facilitates this process.

Where appropriate, the checklist also facilitates a comparison between actual and budgeted/forecast figures (for example, time input; costs), to provide a constant check on actual performance against expected performance

Subjective evaluation

If we accept that client satisfaction derives largely from perceived effectiveness, it is necessary to find out about client perceptions, and the most obvious method of doing so is to ask!

The subjective questionnaire in Appendix 4 was developed as a complementary tool, to be used in conjunction with the objective checklist.It comprises open-ended, non-directive questions, which seek to elicit the precise opinions/feelings of the client. A more specific form of questionnaire used alone could not achieve this; in imposing a framework on the client, it might completely fail to identify what are, for them, the most salient issues. The questionnaire is a tool by which to assess the client's level of satisfaction at any point in time – as it were, taking the temperature of the water. It provides information which can be acted upon immediately

To monitor the evaluation process in this way is similar to the internal audit process – a monitoring of the control process. As such, it is desirable organisational practice.

This questionnaire, together with the checklist, can be used as frequently as is thought necessary – half-yearly, quarterly or monthly. The optimal frequency depends upon a number of factors; for example, length of contract or size of fee income. It can be used with one or more key people in the client organisation, perhaps at different levels. For example, the chief executive, the marketing manager and the marketing executive with responsibility for PR activities should be involved.

A significant problem which must be recognised is that these key people do not remain constant, and are replaced by new individuals with their own perceptions. The questionnaire might usefully be used shortly after a new key executive joins the client organisation.

Research has shown that as the relationship between consultant and client develops over time, so too does the level of tact

85

used in that relationship. The client finds it increasingly difficult and ultimately impossible to confront the consultant with his or her dissatisfaction. They are too friendly! In the end the client can only cope with this situation by terminating the relationship abruptly. There are two possible solutions to this:

(a) the consultant and client talk out the problems in an extended interview lasting several hours, after which time tactful conventions can hopefully be overcome; or

(b) the use of a third party intermediate.

Once the client's perceptions are known, and an objective evaluation of the effectiveness of the relationship has been made, suggestions for improvement should of course be made in close consultation with the client.

The same strictures apply to initial proposal presentation. A participative development of the brief solves many of the problems which would otherwise arise later on, were the consultant's preferences simply to be imposed without consideration upon the client.

Activity records

Appendix 4 sets out a suggested format for an activity record. This provides basic data to help the evaluation process. A similar reporting format is often used for costs/expenses.

The problem in implementing this kind of system is that form-filling is always an irksome task. For this reason 'Activity Record' is preferable to, for example 'Time Sheet'.

Such a system cannot be successfully used unless it is participative. All those involved must understand and accept the benefits. The system must also be effectively monitored. For example, directors must ensure that accurate records are being properly kept. Keeping an accurate record of the deployment of human resources is becoming increasingly important, as their value increases.

A large sweets manufacturer asked its travelling salespeople, over a period of six months, to record their activities every half hour, the objective being to discover exactly how they spent their time. Most efficient organisations accept the importance of 'activity reports'.

The specimen form in Appendix 4 can be used in various ways:

1. The sheets can be filled in as an on-going activity, simply ticking across the page as each activity takes place, or they can be completed retrospectively, eg daily or weekly. the former method is more reliable.

2. Each day records 30 incidents. Research shows this to be sufficient for most executives. The numbers in the lefthand margin denote each separate incident.

3. The list of headings given in this specimen form is exhaustive. One could select only those which appear to be most appropriate and useful.

4. A sensible approach might be to conduct a small pilot study using the specimen activity record for a brief period, after which it could be reviewed and modified on the basis of experience. Such an experimental period would also yield extremely valuable data about the deployment of resources within the organisation.

5. It is recommended that senior executives should keep this record themselves for an initial period – say one week – to gauge whether it is (a) feasible and (b) useful.

Chapter 6

Success and Failure in PR

As has been seen in earlier chapters, some personality types are simply not suited to the demands of public relations, while others seem to have a natural flair for the work – be it attributable to their empathetic qualities, interest in people, positive attitudes or 'butterfly minds', or, indeed, to a combination of all of these qualities. However, the work of even the most brilliantly talented person will be seriously impaired by lack of organisation.

Good basic organisation cannot remove the problems caused by sudden eruptions in the workload or by mini-crises, but it provides a framework for coping with the routine, so that sudden problems can be better handled. Sound organisation may be very attractive to potential clients and it helps the establishment of a new account without detracting from existing work.

There are special problems inherent in public relations: the delicate relationships between the individual and the organisation, between one client and another, between systems control and creative innovation, between overreacting and underreacting. In essence, the key to successful and effective public relations lies precisely in getting these balances just right. It is all a question of judgement. To put this another way, one can make a comprehensive list of conditions which are necessary to good public relations, but these conditions would never be sufficient to guarantee success, unless the balance was right.

This statement has important and far-reaching implications for the education and training of public relations practitioners. While formal education and training, whether academic or

practical 'on-the-job', may aim to inculcate a proper understanding and appreciation of the conditions required for successful PR, such methods of teaching cannot ensure that the
student develops the necessary judgement and sensitivity. This
is really a question of learning to learn, which can only be done
through experience – although, of course, that experience may
be distilled, simulated and, to some extent, accelerated.

LEARNING TO LEARN

The simplest type of system is closed and mechanical. Imagine
the workings of a thermostat. The temperature gauge is set at
70°F. During the evening, the actual room temperature falls
below this level. An automatic feedback process operates,
igniting the heat source until the temperature of 70°F is once
again reached.

All social systems differ from this model in that they have
the ability to adapt to changes. They are not only able to learn
to do or to be something different in order to fit in and cope
with their changed surroundings, but ultimately they can learn
to learn.

For example, an organisation may learn, through the use of
external consultants, to change to a divisionalised or matrix
company structure. Such a structure may be more appropriate
to the new environmental conditions in which it is operating.
However, operating conditions may, of course, change again,
either reverting to previous patterns or moving on to something new altogether. In this case, the organisation may need
once again to call in the external consultants for advice on how
to adapt its structure. Alternatively, the organisation may be
more sophisticated and have to learn. In which case it may be
able to analyse the new situation and without precedent, devise
a completely new solution.

The same principles apply to both the group and the individual. Individuals can be taught that, for Problem A, they
must implement Solution A; when facing Problem B, they
must implement Solution B. But what are they to do when
problem C appears – which might be similar to A, similar to B,
a combination of factors common to both A and B, or nothing
to do with either of them? It is their inability to learn to learn

Criteria	Vehicle	Personality characteristics	Education	Training	Experience
1 Empathy					
2 Organisational skills					
3 Creativity					
4 Intellect					
5 A grasshopper mind					
6 Motivation					
7 Achievement orientation					
8 General management skills					
9 Stubbornness					
10 Gut instinct					
11 Flair					
12 Rationality					
13 Objectvity					
14 Communication skills					
15 Commitment					
16 Honesty					
17 Perception					
18 Decisiveness					
19 Open-mindedness					
20 Maturity					
21 Balance					
22 Contacts					
23 Optimism					
24 Entrepreneurial flair					

Figure 15
The ideal PR person: checklist of key qualities to be used in staff selection.

which will determine whether or not they are capable of for-
mulating Solution C.

To put this in a public relations context, a particular campaign or strategy may have proven successful in particular circumstances, but cannot be applied to new situations with any
guarantee of success. The key to PR success is the ability to
analyse the new situation, draw comparisons with previous situations, identify any common factors, illuminate any significant differences and, using considerable creative as well as
analytic and diagnostic skill, devise an appropriate and hence
successful solution.

To pursue the analogy with the thermostat, social systems
(organisations, groups, human individuals) have the ability to
modify the goal themselves; to decide to set the regulator at a
lower temperature. So for example, the PR solution, rather
than being seen in terms of the effectiveness of regulators (the
conventional solution) may be reoriented in terms of energy
conservation (the new, original solution).

This is where the creative element of PR can clearly be seen.
Advertising may be more creative in an obvious way, but public relations is more of a craft than an art. The need for, and
opportunities to exploit, lateral thinking are just as real. In fact,
lateral thinking is arguably the key ingredient for ensuring continuing success in the public relations field, and it certainly features in many famous PR campaigns.

TEACHING PEOPLE TO LEARN

Experience is the only effective vehicle for learning the art of
judgement. Experience can, however, be communicated and it
can be distilled. Case studies are one medium for doing this in
formal training.

But undoubtedly the best way to learn to learn is through
real experiences, and a growing – though by no means univer-
sal – trend among PR practitioners is to try and consciously
use experiences as a learning device. The PRCA have produced some case material and CAM lecturers are doing like-
wise as are the PR degree courses.

For an experience to be used effectively as a valuable learning opportunity, the right climate must exist within the group

or organisation. Control and appraisal schemes are specially designed to help learning and to improve and modify behaviour. When a problem arises, its causes can be discussed with all concerned, so that a repetition is avoided.

However, control and appraisal schemes frequently neglect the use of positive rewards and inducements, and rely solely on negative punishments. As a result, risk taking and innovation are discouraged. People prefer to play safe and avoid the risk of being punished, rather than to be innovative and hope for a reward. So it is no use trying to 'set up' experiences as vehicles for individual and organisational learning unless the climate is right. It is important to accept and reward good ideas and intentions, even if these are not immediately successful in implementation. Individuals must feel confident enough to expose their mistakes, so that they and others can learn.

> We get in and we talk about it . . . meetings every two or three weeks. We keep ourselves updated. Perhaps we will take a particular topic, like an audio visual. How successful was it? How many people are asking to see it? How many have seen it once?

> One of the things that came up in the Inquiry was that 16 people had seen a fan sparking. Only two people really had any responsibility and action was taken to ascertain why they had not taken their responsibilities. The very fact is that 16 people saw it. We have over the long term to get a situation where any one of the 16 would have said: 'Christ, that fan is sparking. . . .' and done something about it.

Chapter 7

Crisis Situations

Crises such as Chernobyl, Three Mile Island or Seveso, air disasters, oil rig blow outs, or even critical strike threats clearly pose special problems in terms of public relations, as do political crises for companies as well as governments. The 'annus horribilis' royal crisis in 1992 and the problems faced by John Major's government in the autumn of 1992 were good examples of the problems of inadequate crisis management.

Is it possible to draw any lessons from the successful handling of public relations in such situations which would be useful in other, more normal, situations? The answer is that certain characteristics of crisis are reflected in a wide range of situations, and there are therefore some valuable lessons to be drawn

Crises provide an interesting context within which to study any kind of organisation process, since behaviour is usually thrown into relief. Extremes can become the norm.

Crises constitute a very real problem in a large number of business and non-profit making concerns. But the literature of management science has to a large extent neglected the subject.

Hermann provided a set of three dimensions with which to define crisis, and this gives us a useful starting point. A crisis:

(a) threatens high priority values of the organisation;
(b) presents a restricted amount of time in which a response can be made;
(c) is unexpected or unanticipated by the organisation.

The degree to which each of these descriptions applies varies between different types of crisis. It can also be said that a crisis may develop in response to a change of some kind in the operating environment, or it may be internally generated (see Figure 16).

	Internally generated	Caused by a change in the environment
Threatens high priority values of the organisation		
Presents a restricted amount of time in which a response can be made		
Unexpected or unanticipated by the organisation		

Figure 16
Checklist of types of crisis

REACTIONS TO CRISIS

One of the most interesting research findings is that, when facing a crisis situation, managers may react in very restrictive ways. Unfortunately, such behaviour may not prove to be in the best interests of the organisation. When facing a financial crisis, for instance, many managers tighten up control systems and increase the frequency of reporting procedures. However, such behaviour results in the loss or filtering of vital information about what is going on outside the organisation, to which it should be responding.

The critical balance, which is so difficult to achieve, is to ensure a full appreciation of the realities of the situation and its potential seriousness, and to respond in a calm and rational way; and not to panic.

The public relations function is of paramount importance in a crisis. It provides the interpretation of events to which everyone, inside and outside the organisation concerned, will react. In other words, the PR people are influencing, maybe even shaping, other people's perceptions and hence responses.

Most of the experienced PR practitioners interviewed for this book have emphasised that one of the keys to effective public relations is knowing when to react and when not to. They believe that overreacting can do more damage than leaving the thing alone. The PR head of one of the former nationalised industries, explained his own philosophy: 'Today's newspapers, after all, are only tomorrow's fish and chip wrapping.' He maintains that that is a healthy attitude to the press:

> If you worry too much about the press and about what they are saying about you . . . you would never sleep at night. You would never sleep.

However, he also thinks that this is one of the most difficult things to teach new staff, and probably can only be acquired through experience. As a simple operating rule, he advises:

> I think on balance if you are in doubt you should not respond. At least not respond directly, but try and find some other way of making a point or get somebody else to make the point for you.

Indeed, the PR chief of another large industrial concern, who recently moved into the PR function from marketing responsibilities within the same organisation, agrees on the importance of knowing when to react, but says:

> That is something which I certainly have not fully learned yet, and I have to feel my way along this; but I get good advice from my staff on this.

PREDICTABLE AND UNPREDICTABLE CRISES

One of the dimensions useful in defining a crisis concerns the question of whether it was unexpected or unanticipated by the organisation. One has to identify, first, the processes through which the organisation becomes aware of the problem or crisis, and, second, the processes through which it responds and adapts to the need for change. The difference between these processes is critically important, since it distinguishes those crises which are totally unanticipated from those crises which, although privately recognised as being imminent, are not for some time either publicly acknowledged or proactively managed. It seems necessary to include the latter within any definition of crisis in the context of business organisations, since it is not an unusual phenomenon. Indeed, it has been suggested that imminent crisis are often apparent within the organisation for up to 12 months – this being the period for disclosing financial data – before being accepted and publicly announced.

In an organisation there are obvious reasons for such reticence. In the case of the individual, this kind of behaviour can be explained in terms of psychological stress: feelings of anxiety and insecurity lead, ultimately, to the withdrawal syndrome.

The banking industry provides an excellent example of the importance of PR. The whole system is based on confidence and trust, and the role of the PR person is to keep those in the best possible condition. This role extends through the whole process, from realisation of the crisis, to acceptance of it, and then to guiding and projecting the organisation's response. It is not too ambitious to suggest that PR might well develop as a discipline to the point where it is helping to analyse the organisation, and to identify possible problem areas and so avert potential crises.

Figure 17 gives a wider working definition of crisis which provided the theme for the advertisement reproduced in Figure 18.

It can be argued that public relations has a role to play in risk management. Calculated risks in statistical terms are not possible, since a risk is a risk and cannot be controlled by measurement. Nevertheless, management must organise to be in a position to cope effectively with crises, or emergency situations, whether predicted or unpredicted, accepted or ignored.

The organisation is:

	RESPONDING	NOT RESPONDING
The organisation is:		
AWARE	1	2
NOT AWARE	4	3

1 – Aware and responding
2 – Aware but not responding
3 – Neither aware nor responding
4 – Not aware but responding nevertheless (?)

Figure 17
Predictable and unpredictable crises

EXAMPLES OF THE PR ROLE IN CRISIS SITUATIONS

The critical question in crisis situations is always how much information should be given.

> Our role is to get authoritative information out as quickly as possible. Our problem is that the management and the people who know the facts are busy striving to organise a rescue, but we know that if we do not give positive, on the spot information as quickly as possible, the press would go and get it from Charlie's cousin who works in a greengrocer's shop or something like that . . . and it will become garbled and perhaps more horrific than it need be. So we have somehow to try and persuade management to brief the press quickly and authoritively.

Similarly:

> I think we have an obligation to tell the public the facts in non-emotive terms. Not to conceal things, because there is the argument that if you tell them too much you frighten them; there is also the argument that if you do not tell them

Figure 18

anything you frighten them even more. And our job is to see that the facts are not distorted, and if you try to withhold them the distortion sets in.

Contingency planning

A broad range of potential crises and disaster situations can in fact be covered by elaborate contingency plans.

There is, for example, for every electricity authority or generating authority a crisis plan for dealing with a nuclear alert. But it has never been used, because actually power stations are incredibly safe.

There was one crisis where a power station looked as if it might blow up and scatter the area around with coal dust. But it did not happen. At the end of the day I suppose you could say we alerted people unnecessarily.

Contingency planning depends upon a rigorously logical consideration of all possible events and, with added complexity, all possible combinations of events and their consequences. Most contingency plans are never put to the test, of course, though there are practical exceptions:

Unfortunately, there have been far too many of these incidents in the past, and so we have a certain amount of experience, and we have worked out a certain amount of drill.

Emergency organisation

All the people who are directly responsible for handling the public relations function in a crisis or emergency situation describe contingency plans which establish very similar organisations to cope with the immediate problems. In every case the PR chief remains at head office, sending a senior person to the site as quickly as possible. Where necessary, he or she is assisted by people co-opted in from other areas near to the site. All emphasise the importance of this spokesperson being able to speak with authority; they have to have some 'clout', they have to 'be able to boss the press as well ... to stop the press getting in the way of the rescue operation'. This is recognised as a difficult job for the person on the spot, and invariably he or she will have undergone intensive television training.

The PR chief is usually responsible for coordination.

The chap on the spot is having briefing sessions, press conferences, arranging interviews for television, that sort of thing, but he never sees what comes out. So one of my functions is to keep an eye on the box and radio and tell him what has been said and if something has been said which is misleading or damaging, to try and put it right.

. . . we agree a brief, and this is all linked up to London with radio communications.

We have to avoid using the services that are going to be needed for the rescue operation, for example, telephone, things like that.

We have video equipment so that all television programmes, and radio programmes, are monitored and we have our own VTRs of them, so we know exactly what was said and what was done and we can get a consistent line. We have land line conference facilities, so we are in constant contact, so the whole thing is geared up on a fairly sophisticated basis.

The critical coordinating role of the PR chief is recognised explicitly in many organisations. Often, for example, under emergency conditions, he or she is able to specify what resources must be allocated to cope with the situation; he or she advises the chief executive about resource allocation. It is often indeed the PR department which receives information about the crisis before the rest of the management hierarchy, since

the press and news agencies are in business to get information quickly, are they not? And so quite often we get a call from maybe a local agency man who has been tipped off that ambulances have been called to a certain site.

Within that particular organisation, this informal channel of communication had been recognised officially, so that while during working hours the normal hierarchical communication structure operates, outside office hours the official line of communication is through the PR department.

Lessons to be learned

The military model is still used for organisation efficiency. Under conditions of extreme danger inefficiencies will tend to be minimised. Certain lessons do appear from what has been said about the establishing of emergency organisations: clear lines of communication, coordination to achieve consistency of information, the risks of misinformation filling any vacuums.

Several people comment on the relationship between the PR team and the press and other media, during crises. The PR person on the spot necessarily has a special role to play and a special relationship with the press; he or she has to 'boss' the media; in other words, his or her relationship is probably more effective.

> I think that the heat of the moment often engenders a greater degree of understanding between the media and us ... a much greater level of understanding and cooperation. It is a much healthier situation in fact than you get generally speaking with a serious TV programme, like 'World in Action' or 'Panorama', because they may have been motivated by some pressure group. Now in an incident situation something has actually happened, men are dead, for instance. There is less chance of dishonesty, there is a much greater relationship. We have had a couple of rough deals ... but never on incidents, only on issues.

The UK government's handling of the Iraq arms crisis, the Royal Family's handling of the marriage problems of the Duke and Duchess of York and the Prince and Princess of Wales, together with the on-going crisis of confidence in the Major government in the winter of 1992, all illustrate the importance of crisis management.

Chapter 8

How to Survive: the Dilemma of the PR Consultancy

The recession of the early 1990s has caused convulsions in the UK and international PR industry. However, beyond the question of immediate survival lies the issue of growth. Is there an optimal size for a PR operation, or indeed for any other kind of entrepreneurial organisation? Most PR companies are small but this leads to problems such as deciding where best to channel profits. On the other hand, companies which decide to go for growth, and to overcome any inherent constraints on growth which exist, face the following questions:

- how to find new business

- how best to fit new business into the existing organisation structure

- how to keep new business.

THE GROWTH PATTERN OF ORGANISATIONS

There are three stages of corporate development:

- pioneering

- specialisation

- integration.

The transition from the pioneering stage to specialisation is particularly problematic, for this marks the critical turning point in the career of the entrepreneur: the point at which he or she must decide either to stand still (which strategy may in fact prove impossible) or to opt for continued development, which requires organisation.

The essential functions for any organisation are:

- maintenance
- adaptation
- goal attainment
- integration.

Where one or more of these is not met, an organisation is unlikely to survive on its own. Successful entrepreneurs manage all four functions themselves, until they opt for company growth. The key problems typically facing the entrepreneur at this stage include:

- how to structure the organisation in the face of increasing size – specifically, how to delegate the processes of decision making
- how to structure the organisation so that it is effective at both the routine maintenance and the adaptive functions.

Many entrepreneurs never manage this transition. Hence the proliferation of one-person outfits in public relations. Companies going through the transition from a 'man, a boy and a dog' operation to a larger organisation are very often bedevilled by personnel problems. Frequent and unanticipated changes in personnel create a series of crisis points. The cause of such crises can usually be traced back to one or more of the following:

- Inadequate control
- ambiguous roles
- centralised decision making.

Recovery and continued development is often dependent upon the company obtaining larger, more stable accounts, which give greater continuity of personnel, successful delegation of various aspects of the business and improved controls.

Increasing size tends to lead to greater formalisation of roles.

This ensures continuity and stability and reduces ambiguity, but at the same time it reduces flexibility and the expression of individual personalities. Hence the tendency for PR agencies to remain small. Regimentation is incompatible with individual responsibility and creative implementation. Similarly, as size increases, so decisions are decentralised. But which decisions to decentralise and to whom?

Very often a major stumbling block – for strong psychological reasons – is the recruiting of an effective number-two person to the entrepreneur. In organisation terms, the problem really hinges on the need to differentiate between routine, operational activities, and longer-term, strategic, adaptive thinking and planning, and then the need to integrate the two.

Specialisation versus coordination is, perhaps *the* key problem of organisation design (see Chapter 2), and is never more prominent than at this stage in a company's development. Only if some system such as work groups or teams or 'organisational families' can be made viable, can an organisation at the pioneering stage in its development hope to progress effectively to the integration stage and in so doing bypass the intermediate stage of specialisation.

EVALUATING NEW BUSINESS

Development of the company reaches a point where the successful entrepreneur must be selective in the new business they accept. There are sound organisation and business reasons, for example, for attracting only compatible types of business and developing a clearly visible distinctive competence in specific areas, quite apart from the obvious risks of taking on business which is bad from a financial point of view.

Following are some suggested criteria for the evaluation of new business opportunities and new business proposals.

They are not intended to be comprehensive, but should provide a useful basis for discussion and elaboration.

Clearly some criteria will be given greater importance than others. The problem is how to compile an overall assessment using these criteria as a framework.

Distinctive competence

The first problem is to define the distinctive competence of the company or PR department. Does this relate to the way in which it runs campaigns? Or to dealing with specific types of business/industry?

New business opportunities can be evaluated using the following questions:

1. Is the distinctive competence appropriate for the new business?

2. Is the new business complementary to existing business? If not, does the necessary diversification follow in a logical direction for it, and one that could lead to further business in the new area?

3. Will the new business enhance or weaken corporate image?

4. Is the company/department currently organised to be able to take on the new business effectively, without risk to existing business, within the time scale envisaged?

5. Is it probable that the new business will satisfy its profitability requirement (eg 20 per cent)?
   Note: a minimum fee could be established (eg £20,000 pa), below which the potential profitability of the new business (ie level of return as compared with level of resource input) would be very carefully scrutinised.

6. Is there a possibility of the new business creating further new business opportunities, eg a one-off assignment leading to an on-going relationship; work for one company leading to relationships with other associated, subsidiary or parent companies?

7. What is the growth potential of the specific new business opportunity? What factors will affect the development of this potential, and to what extent can changes in those factors be forecast?

8. What is the possibility of the client delaying/defaulting in payments to the company?

9. What is the reason for the new business opportunity presenting itself?

Why does the client want to retain the company? Is this acceptable to the company?

Evaluating acceptable proposals

While it is probably not necessary, or even desirable, to stipulate a uniform formula for new business proposals, it is useful to draw up a checklist of criteria for evaluating acceptable proposals. A clearly recognisable house style also helps the professional appearance of proposals.

Such a list of criteria for evaluation might include the following:

1. Format. The proposal should have a logical structure which is clearly set out on the contents page. It should be concise, lucid and generally well written. A well spaced layout not only improves the appearance of the document but also facilitates ease and speed of reading; appropriate emphases and the flow of the argument are also more obvious. When used selectively, statistics can indicate a good research input. Detailed statistics, presented as clearly as possible, are best relegated to an appendix. Where it is necessary to introduce some figures into the text, these are most easily interpreted if presented in diagrammatic or graphical form.

2. A good proposal should state specifically:

   (a) The objectives of the proposed activity. these stated objectives should seek to answer the following questions:

   - What is the message to be communicated?

   - To whom is this message to be communicated?

   - How is this message to be communicated?

   - What will happen as a result of this message being communicated and received by this audience?

   (b) The methods which will be used to achieve those objectives.

(c) The deployment of resources – time input, financial resources etc; specifically, how resources will be allocated to
- client liaison
- press liaison
- special events
- planning
- reporting
- miscellaneous

(d) The methods used by the company or department to evaluate and review on-going PR activity.

3. Except in special cases (eg renewal or expansion of existing business) it may be useful to argue generally for the role of PR, and specifically to demonstrate the relevance and potential benefit to the client company of PR activity. The proposal might include some brief comment on the effectiveness of external PR agencies as compared with in-house PR departments.

4. A professional proposal should also indicate, if not demonstrate, a knowledge of the client's industry and of his particular organisation. If possible, it should illustrate how PR activity could help solve some key problems currently facing the client.

5. Some indication of the company or PR department's distinctive competence should be given. In which ways is it a preferable alternative to other PR companies which might be submitting competitive proposals?

6. It is important from the point of view of credibility to give potential clients a clear indication of (a) the current portfolio of clients with, if appropriate, renewal rates, and (b) the organisation and flexibility of available resources within the company. It is a debatable point whether it is best to include this information in the proposal itself, or as some kind of attached prospectus. The best strategy tends to vary according to the individual case.

CASE STUDY

The best way of understanding the problems involved in fitting new business into an existing organisation structure is to use a specific example. We consider here how PR Consultants Ltd prepared itself to receive prospective new business accounts.

Two points were established at the outset as being crucial to the search for a solution

1. Any modification of the existing organisation structure must be made with an awareness of the processes involved. The structure should make easier the smooth running of the company.

2. Certain basic assumptions had to be questioned and challenged, and not be automatically incorporated in new structure proposals.

PRC Ltd's existing organisation structure

The structure of the organisation before any changes were made is illustrated in Figure 19. The first stage in looking at the possibilities of reorganisation was a role analysis exercise. The usefulness of this exercise was that by focusing on each individual's role within the organisation, it related structure and process and highlighted any mismatch between the two. Focusing on the dynamic aspects of the organisation's activities, this approach also identified those basic assumptions which needed to be questioned. This approach reflected a professional disaffection with the imposed package solutions favoured by many of the larger management consulting firms.

Three problem areas were identified:

1. *The role of Number Two to the Chairman*
    The Number Two's role appeared to be perceived, both by himself and by the Chairman, as that of (a) Managing Director Elect and (b) Manager of Group A. Role (a) would imply some kind of authority over the other directors, but as yet this relationship appeared ambiguous, and some future conflict was inevitable. Overt (as opposed to covert) conflict had so far been avoided simply because there had been no need for the two groups to coordinate in this way.

Current proposals seemed to mean that Number Two would be displaced by a new Group Managing Director who might be less able to cope with that role. The question to be asked here was whether the founder would really prefer to limit his own role to that of Chairman, or whether he envisaged developing his role more as that of Chief Executive.

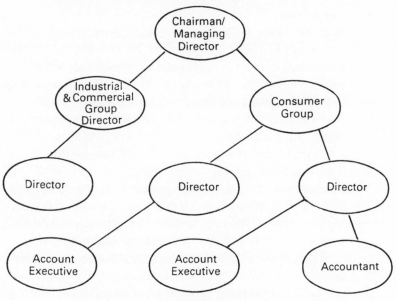

Figure 19
PRC Ltd's existing organisation structure

2. *Bases for divisional split*

The company was divided, according to type of client, into Consumer and Industrial accounts and Commercial accounts. The basic assumption to be questioned here concerned the criteria used to split the company in this way. Do the different types of activity require distinctive competences? If so, is it logical to structure the organisation on this basis? Or is this distinction artificial? Would it be more logical to divide the company on the basis of clients/accounts?

The existing intention to place new consumer business under the aegis of the industrial and commercial group would have led to an organisation structure divided on the basis of type of activity and client/account. This would have been ambiguous and confusing. Consider, for example, the position of X in Figure 20: to whom should he be responsible?

The acquisition of significant business which blurred the traditional divide emphasised the urgent need to define the criteria to be used in structuring the organisation.

3. *Integration*

Role relations showed a hierarchical structure. Most importantly, there appeared to be virtually no cross-functional communication at any level, from the directors downwards, although vertical relationships and communications appeared to be satisfactory. This communications pattern probably developed because previously all members of the staff had related to the Chairman/Managing Director on a one-to-one basis. The need for lateral communications was becoming increasingly important, as for example, the X account and the Y account failed to fall neatly within the existing divisions of the organisation. Integration would also help generate new business from existing accounts.

Who should perform this integration function? Should coordination be channelled through the Chairman/Managing Director? Through the Group Managing Directors? Or through their staff?

Drawbacks of the existing structure of PRC Ltd

At the level of the Management Committee, lateral communications appeared to be weak, and as a result the role of the Committee appeared limited. There were a number of possible explanations for this, for example:

(a) highly centralised control by the Chairman/Managing Director;

(b) lack of appreciation of the need for lateral communications;

(c) too little time because of high work pressure.

The terms of reference for the Management Committee probably also needed to be amplified

There was also a need for improved communication and

coordination mechanisms at all levels in the organisation below the Management Committee.

Proposed reorganisation of PRC Ltd

The new structure which was proposed is illustrated in Figure 20. Although one of several directors reporting directly to the Chairman/Managing Director, the Number Two would be primus inter pares, deputising where necessary. Other Groups would, however, work laterally with Number Two.

This structure would facilitate further organised expansion within the usual range of activities, or the diversifying of the company into consultancy activities. It also offered the possibility of setting up separate functions; for example, finance and accounting, personnel, and administration, if the company continued to grow to a point at which separation of line and staff seemed preferable.

The new structure would put the company in a position to exploit new business opportunities which arose as a result of work in one Group, but which offered future work within the scope of another Group.

A number of recommendations were made:

1. The development of more lateral processes at all levels within the company; improved horizontal communications and coordination. For example: improve the effectiveness of management meetings and amplify their terms of reference; use of information exchanges between Groups; suggested areas of possible cooperation.

2. Where a specific account falls into more than one Group or does not fall logically into any of them, a possible solution would be to elect a project coordinator on an ad hoc basis. Such an arrangement allows far greater flexibility than the establishing of an elaborate matrix or project organisation, though maintaining the balance between flexibility and ambiguity remains a very complex task.

3. Task forces could be set up to process new business propositions. A task force is temporarily superimposed on the functional structure, and is used to short-circuit communication lines in times of high uncertainty.

111

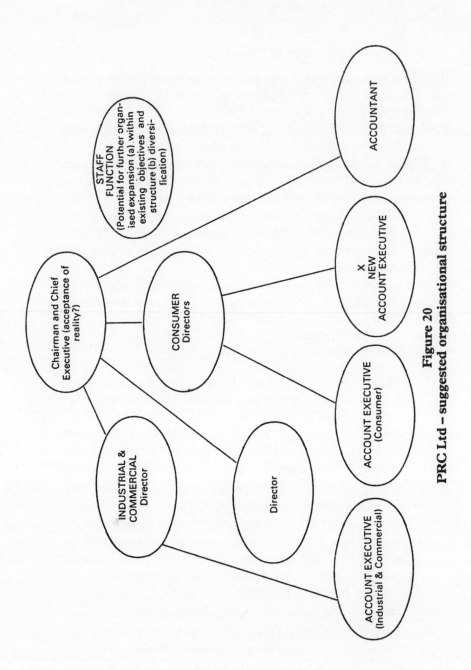

Figure 20
PRC Ltd – suggested organisational structure

When the uncertainty decreases, the functional hierarchy resumes its guiding influence.

Such task forces have the following advantages:

(a) they increase flexibility:

(b) they are temporary, and are dissolved as soon as the problem or task is solved;

(c) they give increased responsibility to individuals without a concomitant and necessarily permanent increase in status;

(d) problems are removed from higher levels in the hierarchy and can be solved at quite low levels in the organisation.

They only work, however, if people behave in a confronting, problem-solving manner.

4. Increase in scope the role of staff personnel. Specifically, increase centralisation of the financial control function. This would:

(a) facilitate greater control over profitability;

(b) provide a much needed integrative function between the various groups within the company, enabling it to function more as a cohesive organisation. The integrator role, to be effective, must have credibility with all groups in the company and be seen to be unbiased. The effectiveness of this role is increased by the amount of supporting factual information available; for example, an information system reporting actual expenditures against functional or departmental budgets. This role is in fact very difficult; it is suggested that it would initially require the overt support of the Chair-man/Managing Director to give it credibility.

This is not to suggest that the autonomy of the various group managers should be reduced with regard to financial planning and control within their own group budgets. But, as a profit centre, each group would operate within a better defined and centrally controlled framework of financial objectives.

5. Encourage more active role negotiation, specifically

between (a) the Chairman/ Managing Director and other company directors, and (b) directors managing separate groups within the company. The point here is that the ambiguity and potential conflict must be resolved on a lateral basis; ie, an appeal to higher authority is unsatisfactory in that this leaves unresolved the basic points of contention. It is infinitely preferable for such negotiation to be carried out in an open, honest manner. This increases the general level of trust within an organisation.

6. Exposure of key personnel to current thinking in the area of organisational behaviour. It is suggested that this is most profitable if the learning experience is shared with other members of the role set or work group.

RECENT DEVELOPMENTS AND FUTURE TRENDS

During the 1980s, the PR industry grew at a phenomenal pace. In 1986 *The Economist* reported that the industry had grown at the rate of 48 per cent, making it the fastest growing sector of the UK economy. Since then the growth has slowed down due to the recession. As one leading practitioner, Reginald Watts, said in 1992:

> The public relations industry has passed through two years of catharsis. Many good consultancies have hit the wall and some undercapitalised ones have merged. But one factor stands out. The industry will never be the same again.

During the 1980s, the publicly quoted PR conglomerate emerged to dominate the PR business. The rise and fall of some of these companies has highlighted the weakness of the management function in many of these fast growing organisations.

At the start of this period of dynamic change a number of companies vied for top position. The Good Relations Group plc was the first to seek and obtain a full listing on the Stock Exchange in 1983. It was the largest PR organisation in the UK between 1982 and 1986. It aimed to challenge the supremacy of Hill and Knowlton (the subsidiary of J Walter Thompson) and Burson Marsteller as the world's largest. In 1984 the Good Relations Group was at its peak with anticipated profits of £1.3m for that year. But on 23 December 1984 an article in the *Sunday Telegraph* (headlined 'Poor Relations') reported on the rumour that the company planned to close their recently opened City office. The City editor forecast that this would lead to the loss of staff and clients. The following day the shares, then standing at an all time high of 280, fell 100p; a Stock Exchange record fall for one day. On 30 August 1985, seven months later, Maureen Smith, the Chief Executive and architect of Good Relations' growth, left the company. The well publicised difficulties both before and after her departure have highlighted the volatility of the PR service business.

Between 1986 and 1989 the Shandwick Group became the largest independent PR company in the world. By 1992 it was facing the biggest crisis in PR history, with its share prices plunging to a low of 5p. The situation has changed dramatically for many other companies too.

Leading PR companies in the UK

1989	1992
Shandwick	Shares fall to 5p (December)
Charles Barker	Goes into liquidation (management buy-out)
Burson Marsteller	Remains steady despite drastic cutbacks
Dewe Rogerson	Remains steady and develops internationally
The Grayling Company	Part of large Lopex plc. Shares under pressure
Hill & Knowlton	Part of WPP. Reorganises after client cutbacks
Valin Pollen	Liquidated in 1988
Broad St	Liquidated
Countrywide	Steady
Good Relations	Merged into Lowe Bell Communications
D J Edleman	Steady
Kingsway Rowland	Reorganises after client cutbacks
Paragon Communications	Sold to Shandwick

With the demise of Vallin Pollen and Broad Street, Brunswick has risen rapidly to lead the pack of corporate communications consultancies specialising in merger and acquisition work.

The two biggest problems facing the PR industry in the early 1990s have been the recession and the lack of effective management and training. The dearth of managers and well-trained executives inhibited the growth of consultancies and undermined the stability of many established companies. The demand for PR specialists in the heady 1980s had made PR head-hunting a new opportunity for the recruitment businesses.

One of the weakest features of the public relations business is the lack of management skills in running the companies themselves. On 6 January 1987 the *Financial Times* reported:

> Ten directors quit PR company – the resignations yesterday of 10 directors of one of Britain's fastest-growing public relations companies stem from serious boardroom differences that seem to be symptoms of a deeper malaise affecting PR industry as a whole

There is nothing new in the 'deeper malaise affecting the PR industry as a whole' as reported by David Churchill of the *Financial Times*. It stems from the fact that buccaneering individuals who initially succeeded in establishing successful PR consultancies have little or no experience of the management requirements for running a large company. In most cases the structures they establish are inappropriate to the 'task culture' requirements of the PR function. Inevitably as the structures become overloaded and bureaucratic they cease to function. In addition, during the recession, Broad Street, Streets, Charles Barker and many medium-sized and small companies bit the dust. Few had built up resources and, once the economic effects of the slump were felt, they fell victim.

On a small scale, the industry is facing the problems that have fuelled the management debate about the multinational conglomerates. Professor Michael Porter of the Harvard Business School, author of *Competitive Strategy* and *Competitive Advantage* focus on the practical choices open to businesses in building the web of strategic alliances they need and highlights the role that the PR practitioner can play in the new era of multinational organisations.

What is clear is that the PR quoted companies will only be able to maintain their status as growth companies by using their 'paper' to acquire more companies. But the lessons that have been learnt from recent experience in the PR 'people' business, is that the organisation will only remain in tact if the operating companies retain their original ecologies. Centralisation of functions like accounts or exercising central control over management decisions will lead to disenchantment and continuing breakaways. The organismic flair of the 'task culture' will not be maintained by changing the cultures.

This lesson probably lay at the heart of the early success of the Saatchi & Saatchi Group and WPP. However, the decline of profits after ten years' continuous growth in 1989 highlighted Saatchi's difficulty in maintaining the 'task cultures' in their worldwide business.

A similar philosophy lay behind the extraordinary growth of the WPP Group led by Martin Sorrell, former finance director of Saatchi & Saatchi. By 1990, WPP had become the largest international marketing services group with the acquisition of Ogilvy & Mather, which joined J Walter Thompson, and an impressive range of other acquisitions.

WPP adopted as a basic tenet of their business philosophy that each acquisition must remain independent and continue to operate in the market niche it had established. The founders and existing management teams were motivated by further tranches of 'buy-out' cash if they grew by 20 per cent per annum and maintained a 20 per cent profit margin. Their executives were given incentives in the form of share options and profit sharing. The culture that brought the company its early success through 'non-interference' clauses in the acquisition agreement, ran into difficulties as the former owners left.

The PR industry in the early 1990s is not likely to grow substantially while the recession continues. A new generation of consultancies is already developing with special niche markets as a direct result of the recession, while the list of casualties and bankruptcies increases. As one leading practitioner says:

> Gone for good is the vagueness and mystique that beset so many PR campaigns in the past. In their place will be more precision, more pre-testing of messages and above all more communications programmes that contain task-driven activities with objectives that are quantifiable not just for exposure but for impact as well.

The completion of the internal market in 1992 presented a further important new dimension for public relations practices. Specialist agencies able to operate across European countries could be attractive to multinational organisations. There will be a continuing growth of specialist consultancies, particularly in the areas of strategic positioning, public affairs, and issue, crisis and events management. In addition:

> Senior managers will demand from their public relations practitioners programmes that combine the data-base skills of the direct marketing world with the sophistication of the advertising media planner. Within five years we can expect the mobile personal communicators to have reached a level of usage whereby public relations professionals will network into software that gives them data on target audiences of such detail that the messages and delivery systems will make the average advertising campaign of today look like a blunderbuss. Our programmes, whether we like it or not, will make some of the techniques described in George Orwell's novel *1984* look like children's games.

Another important development which took place in 1987 affected the attitudes of the PR directors of the larger consultancies. Under the terms of the Companies Act, directors of companies are personally liable for any debts incurred by the company should it fail. This was a new and onerous responsibility and for directors of PR companies which have not matured or developed a proper financial information system, can be a source of considerable concern. It could also provide a further incentive for breakaways from large companies. It has certainly been a focus for public debate as a result of the collapse of a number of leading PR agencies.

The future growth of the PR industry looks assured but most practitioners recognise the new challenges:

> Only those practitioners who come to terms with this harder-nosed approach by the new generation of business managers will survive. What the economic down-turn has done is to make managers examine the soft elements of management such as human resources and public relations and ask questions like 'What are the benefits?'

> Consultant and in-house practitioners alike need to develop new ways of working which are less like the old supplier and buyer relationship and more like the Japanese Kieretsu whereby both sides accept a shared destiny, which is tougher to achieve than anything we've known before.

Chapter 9

In-house PR or External Agency?

The issue of whether to use an external public relations consultancy or an internal department has become increasingly relevant. Many organisations are cutting down on internal staff and PR departments are always a target. But the question is often tinged with emotion, and the arguments, on both sides, are often rather more rationalisations than reasons.

In general terms, public relations is the same kind of activity, be it practised by an internal department or an outside concern. There are, nevertheless, significant differences, and these provide arguments for and against, depending upon the particular circumstances.

To illustrate: it may be argued that an external agency can provide a higher degree of objectivity; but, against this, an internal department has access to knowledge and experience of the particular company. Outside contracts may be more expensive; but, against this, the client may feel in a politically more powerful position when it comes to evaluating performance, and the result may well prove ultimately more cost effective. An internal department should, in theory, feel in closer contact with the client and their needs; but intra-organisational relationships often tend, ironically, to be weaker or more problematic than relationships with people outside the organisation. In both types of operation there is a basic client relationship, but, again ironically, in an in-house operation roles may be assumed, taken for granted, with little effort given to defining them properly. Consequently, there may will be more problems of role ambiguity and conflict than in situations where relationships have to be established and developed from base.

A general change is taking place in the way external PR agencies and in-house operations are being used. It would not be true to say that there is – or is likely to be – a swing away from external agencies. Rather, the decision is now tending to be made on the basis of a much more sophisticated appreciation of the real and potential role of public relations, which, as we observed in Chapter 1, is a many-sided activity.

External operations and in-house facilities are now being more appropriately used. Specifically, external agencies are increasingly being used in two types of situation:

(a) where specialist expertise is needed, and this is not available in-house;

(b) as a buffer, where the existing in-hose resources cannot cope with a temporary crisis or peak in demand and workload.

These are precisely the areas where external operations have a distinct competitive advantage. Clearly, external agencies should bear this in mind when considering their own business development programmes.

> I use them both because they are specialists and also to cope with fluctuations.

> Occasionally because the requirement is so specialised that I could not do it without a lot of research, but also when it becomes impossible for me, I cry out and bring them in literally to assist me. But I do not use a full-time public relations consultancy. I do the work that they would do, I do that myself.

The fact that external consultancies charge substantial fees is a frequent objection to their use. But in situations where buffer resources or specialist skills are being bought, the expenditure can be well justified. It has to be seen against the alternatives of making a permanent commitment to cover such situations, or failing to cope when unexpected situations arise.

> For odd things we do use an external agency – to help cope with pressure – but they are more expensive! Very often valuable, though. I think it is necessary to use them. I think it is a matter of circumstances. I think if you are needing to use public relations not long term, you do not want the commitment of someone, then it is fine and valuable.

They make different contributions . . . specialist knowledge.

I think there are times when they are valuable and necessary with work pressures and when they have particular skills which you do not.

There is a further, processual, advantage in using external consultants and this relates back to what was said earlier about the developing and frequently debilitating level of tact in any close working relationship. The outsider brings objectivity to their analysis of the situation, and, equally important, is not barred, psychologically or organisationally, from communicating their analysis and consequent recommendations.

I think often the value of an outside consultancy is to get an outside view which is not an inside one. People look at it objectively, and they can say harsh things which a chappie who has, after all, got to get his salary at the end of the month, cannot afford to say. I think this is often their value, as devil's advocate.

We use the external agency as a sounding board as well.

But of course there is another facet to such objectivity.

Using our own people. I have never dreamt of using consultants. People in the area are going to be affected, and I think have a right to have direct access to the Board and not some consultants.

Particular circumstances will determine which quality is the more critical: objectivity or empathy. Selecting the most appropriate balance between the two is part of the perceptive skill of the public relations specialist. Implementing the right mix is a measure of their organising and managerial ability. This is the art of judgement discussed earlier.

We believe that MPs, newspapers, certainly would get very testy if they found they were dealing with consultants.

But the best consultants are increasingly accepted even in a direct role with these audiences. Overall, there is a growing appreciation of the need for and potential value of public relations activity generally, and of the consultant in particular situations. More and more organisations are reducing their in-house PR operations, as they see the need for well conceived and properly organised public relations activities. PR is no longer seen as something which can reasonably be left to chance, or as a casual adjunct to busy executives' other (primary) concerns.

There is a changing view of the relevance of internal PR departments as opposed to external agencies. In the early 1980s and 1990s, during cutbacks and recession, there was a trend to disband the internal PR department in favour of the external agency. But increasingly there is a more sophisticated understanding of the importance of both. Internal operations are not being set up in order to replace the external agency. Instead the resources needed to manage the PR process effectively are being analysed and, where relevant, the internal and external resources are being upgraded and extended. More appropriate uses of the special skills of the external agency are being assessed. The arguments for a more careful analysis and assessment of the precise needs of the PR function are now recognised. For example, specialist assistance provided externally to undertake a comprehensive 'communications audit' will establish the most cost effective way to achieve defined public relations goals.

In the past few years government departments, privatised industries, local authorities and more recently the Health Service have begun to undertake large-scale audits of their requirements. But the competition to undertake this management consultancy work has increased dramatically. Accountancy firms, management consultants and corporate design consultants, as well as the PR agencies, have been pitching for this lucrative work.

So the scene is undergoing a radical change and the external versus internal resources debate is being replaced by a new scenario. The big questions being faced by the PR practitioner are how to get the maximum impact from the scarce PR resources of manpower; how to structure the PR process to cover the strategic positioning of the organisation in its environment; how to manage the big issues that will determine growth and survival.

Chapter 10

PR Management Training

There are two ways of changing someone's behaviour. You can either change the way they think and behave or you can change their conditions or circumstances so that they are more likely to behave in the way you want.

Similarly, there are two basic approaches to the problem of improving the effectiveness of the public relations function – whether we are talking about an in-house operation or an outside agency. You can either seek to develop the practitioners themselves (management development) or you can work at improving their situation (organisation development).

Combining the two classifications in cube form illustrates the broad range of possibilities for effecting changes with any organisation (see Figure 21). This extends from the use of positive sanctions (rewards) in an attempt to alter a person's intention and hopefully their behaviour, as part of a planned programme of management development (Box A), to the opposite extreme of using negative sanctions (punishments) to seek to alter that person's circumstances so that they are more likely to conform to whatever is required of them, where this is seen as part of an orchestrated attempt to develop the organisation (Box B). Many variations lie in between.

STRATEGY

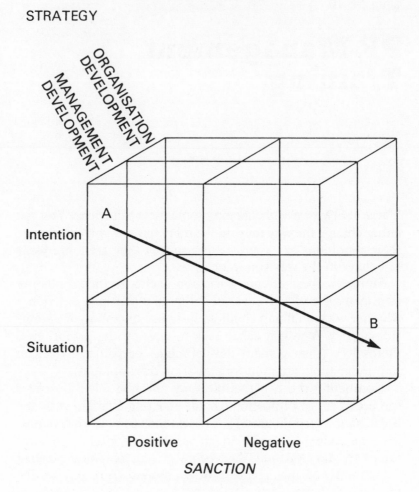

Figure 21
Vehicles for Change

ORGANISATION DEVELOPMENT

The basic problem for all organisations is to resist the inevitable tendency to stagnate. Using the terms introduced in earlier sections, organisations must learn to learn, rather than simply learn; they must be adaptive rather than adapted.

Organisation development (OD) can be characterised as follows:

124

1. It is an educational strategy designed to bring about planned organisation change. At its most simple, this involves a questionnaire/group discussion exercise. More elaborately, group sensitivity training is used. Efforts at change are usually directed at the intervening variables: values, attitudes, relationships and climates, rather than at the end-result variables: the organisation's goals, structure and technology. But it is argued by some that more effective and cheaper efforts might instead focus on those other parts of the system.

2. Most OD programmes are generated by some kind of problem, often crisis, facing the organisation. Changes are therefore directly related to their role in solving that particular problem.

3. The educational philosophy of OD programmes builds on past behaviourial experiences.

4. Change agents are usually brought in from outside the organisation. This preference is explained not only in terms of objectivity but also by the extra political muscle attaching to an outsider.

5. Change agents and clients must work together to achieve success; Bennis uses the word 'collaborate' with care. This is totally dissimilar from the perceived relationship followed by many conventional management consultants.

6. There is an underlying philosophy among professionals involved in OD programmes, and hence discernible in most OD exercises too. For example, organismic organisations are more humane, democratic and ultimately more efficient than bureaucracies. They are concerned with real, authentic relationships, and so with increasing interpersonal skills.

Essentially, organisation development is about choice, and increasing the range of choice at both the individual and the organisational level, so that better decisions can be made in a rapidly changing world.

Two examples of attempts at organisation development and their implications for effective PR behaviour have been given in earlier chapters. Here are three more brief examples taken from the research.

An American bank
We have been pretty flexible in the past. There have been big changes in the Board itself and it has adapted; there was a big reorganisation . . . and minor changes are going on all the time. The structure remains basically the same. The impetus for change typically comes either from myself or the PROs; they are really the key people. We do all the production work and they are the users; they will quickly tell me if I am not providing them with the right gear.

MANAGING CHANGE

An important new dimension for PR practitioners is in the discipline of change management. With re-organisation arriving form privatisation and the re-organisation of the health service, the structure of education and the organisation of government departments and local authorities, the role of managing change has become critical.

A local authority
Well, I am in the process at the moment of having certain organisational changes made. One which we are thinking about at the moment, which has not yet been promulgated and which is not necessarily going to take place, but I hope will, is the subject of greater involvement of local authorities. In order to meet the new requirements the local authorities need to talk to us and need to negotiate with us, and this involves a far greater degree of work and general involvement by a local management which hitherto has not been necessary. They need to produce a total integrated scheme for their area, and you cannot produce a total integrated scheme without us, and on the other hand if they want additional services to the ones that already exist somebody has to pay for them. And the nation will not pay for them through the Department, so that means negotiations and consultations with these people. Local management has to take on this additional responsibility and burden and one part of this responsibility must be communications and public affairs, and PR. And we need to organise ourselves properly in order to cope with that changing requirement. So perhaps that is an example of where our organisation can and must change, in my judgement, to deal with the problems that are facing us at the present time.

The Health and Safety Executive
In organisational terms I think what we need is just two
things. One is the time, the facility to educate inspectors to
understand the issues. A lot of the time we are doing it, but
it is slow, and this is not surprising because they are hard
worked, and we are hard worked, and we do not have time
actually to take them to one side in seminars to teach them.
I think that will undoubtedly come over the long term. Also
relevant to that is the fact that, though they do not realise it,
60 per cent of my branch's function is servicing and 40 per
cent is policy making; though these inspectors do not realise
it, in a few years' time, just as we service them, they will be
servicing us, in execution of PR work. There is that requirement.

The other requirement is a very simple one. It will not
happen in my time, I will not try to make it happen in my
time, but at some stage the Government machinery has to
recognise that the top limit of professionalism has to be
raised in my job. Not in me, in my job. Eventually the status
of communications requirement in PR has to be enhanced
because of the very nature of the job.

Those are the only two things.

MANAGEMENT DEVELOPMENT

Figure 22 compares and contrasts the methods and objectives
of management development with those of organisation development. It would seem that attempts to develop management
potential within public relations are more common than forays
into the world of OD. But which is more effective? Should
investment in management development, at an exponential or
at least increased rate be continued, or should some of these
resources be channelled into organisation development exercises?

Before opting for either of these strategies, the roles of various interested parties must be considered: CAM, PRCA, public relations agencies, in-house PR bosses, the chief executives
of big business and the nationalised industries, academics,
government and the trade unions.

Category	Organisation Development	Management Development
reasons for use	Need to improve overall organisation effectiveness; typical examples of tough problems to be solved: inter-unit conflict; confusion stemming from recent management change; loss of effectiveness due to inefficient organisational structure; lack of teamwork.	Need to improve overall effectiveness of manager; managers do no know company policy or philosophy; managers do not have certain skills; managers seem to be unable to act decisively.
typical goals	To increase the effectiveness of the organisation by: creating a sense of 'ownership' of organisation objectives throughout the workforce; planning and implementing changes more systematically; facilitating more systematic problem solving on the job; to reduce wasted energy and effort by creating conditions where conflict among people is managed openly rather than handled indirectly or unilaterally; to improve the quality of decisions by establishing conditions where	To teach company values and philosophy; to provide practice in management skills which lead to improved organisational effectiveness; to increase ability to plan, coordinate, measure and control efforts of company units to gain a better understanding of how the company functions to accomplish its goals.

decisions are made on the basis of competence rather than organisational role or status;
to integrate the organisation's objectives with the individual's goals by developing a reward system which supports achievement of the organisation's mission as well as individual efforts toward personal development and achievement.

Sending of manager to some educational programme;
job rotation of managers;
specialised training 'packages';

interventions for producing change

education and problem solving is on the job;
learning while problem solving and solving problems while learning following a diagnosis;
utilisation of one or more of the following techniques;

teambuilding
training programmes
inter-group confrontations
data feedback
techno-structural
interventions;

courses and/or conferences;
counselling;
reading of books and articles.

change in organisational structure
job enrichment
change in physical environment
(social architecture).

continued on page 130

129

Category	Organisation Development	Management Development
time frame	Prolonged.	Short, intense.
staff requirements	Diagnostician; catalyst/facilitator; consultant helper; knowledge and skill in the dynamics of planned change; experience in the laboratory method of learning.	Teacher/trainer; programme manager; designer of training programmes; knowledge in the processes of human learning.
values	Humane and non-exploitative treatment of people or organisations; theory Y assumptions; collaboration; sharing of power; rationality of behaviour; openness/candour/honesty; importance of surfacing and utilising conflict; right of persons and organisations to seek a full realisation of their potential; explicitness of values as a value in itself.	Competition; belief that 'education is progress'; belief that managers need challenging periodically; manager's rights to have time for reflection and renewal; belief that individual should 'fit' organisation's need; right of person to seek full realisation of his potential.

Adapted from Burke

Figure 22

A comparison of organisation development and management development

130

THE ROLE OF CAM

The Communication Advertising and Marketing Education Foundation Limited special courses on public relations and marketing communication have had an increasingly high uptake from all sections of industry and the service sector, despite the economic recession. There is evidence to suggest that management is increasingly appreciating the importance of specialised PR training, and this is reflected in the activities of organisations such as the PRCA (Public Relations Consultants' Association), the IPR (Institution of Public Relations) and , of course, the CAM Foundation itself.

CAM actually runs courses in two parts. The Certificate in Communication Studies, which is common to all subsequent Diploma specialisation, is the learning part of the education system and is aimed at providing what CAM calls accelerated experience. The Diploma stage is regarded as the opportunity to apply the knowledge gained at Certificate level to the solution of real life business problems. The full new syllabus is reproduced as Appendix 5 by permission of CAM. People in the public relations industry are happy to have a CAM course qualification. There is no doubt, looking through the guide of the PRCA, that even heads of public relations organisations are identifying themselves more and more readily as having a DipCAM or a Certificate from a CAM course. This is clearly seen to be an important development in the right direction.

It is always possible, however, to criticise. The CAM Foundation offers formal, official training in PR. It also trains marketing and advertising people. There is a great debate going on within the PR industry as to whether this form of training is the right one, because it is felt by some that the disciplines of marketing and advertising are not necessarily relevant to the adequate training of PR people. One of the most effective people on the PR training scene is Frank Jefkins, who has written many books and has proved the value of his practical down-to-earth method of teaching people press relations, how to write a press release, how to meet deadlines, what you do in organising a press conference, how to organise print work, how to run special events, how to mobilise and organise an exhibition stand; all these practical matters are the nitty gritty work of the PR person at junior to middle level. That sort of training is quite different from the training of somebody who is concerned with analysing marketing opportunities.

Marketing people, as well as PR people, should understand the broad context in which the PR function operates, and this is where CAM performs a very important role. The danger is that the course teachers may not be really sure themselves how PR fits in; that can lead to people emerging with a CAM Diploma but not really knowing very much about the PR function. Many such students are frustrated because they do not really feel they have got to grips with the practical problems of PR, even if they are beginning to understand something about the marketing mix.

On the whole the CAM course in PR is making a valiant attempt at encouraging a multidisciplinary approach for those interested in the public relations function. The reason why some PR practitioners are not terribly impressed with the CAM courses in many cases is that they do not seem practical enough in their training. Although an effort has been made to bring in visiting lecturers with practical experience, all too often those who are teaching have very little practical experience of running public relations departments. The problem is that most practitioners are too busy and are not passing on their knowledge to the next generation. Teachers may be people who have not been terribly successful in the practical role.

The missing thing, perhaps, in terms of the public relations programme, is what is covered in more detail under communications practice. The creative aspects, the creative function, involve, according to CAM: the creative interpretation of what is to be communicated to whom, by what media and how; the liaison between the media and the creative production functions; how different media communicate with their audiences; the creative characteristics of the press, television, cinema and other media; how the medium affects the message; and choosing the right kind of message for each medium, and the production techniques that can help communicate it. They also look at the creative task as far as advertising is concerned, not really very much as far as the public relations area is concerned. This may be one of the most important areas for future development.

Creative interpretation is a very difficult subject to teach, but it could be more important than any other area and should at least have a separate paper in the public relations Diploma course. It needs to cover techniques for evaluating and appraising, and how to interpret current political, economic and social trends as they affect some of the specific audiences.

COURSES RUN BY OTHER ORGANISATIONS

If we accept, first that public relations is increasingly being recognised as a specialist activity, and is becoming more visible and sophisticated and, secondly, that there is a growing need for some kind of formal thinking in public relations, what are the best vehicles for organising training?

As we have said CAM plays a central role. There are now a number of UK and US universities offering undergraduate courses in communications, which cover the theory and practice of public relations, marketing and advertising. Cranfield now offer a postgraduate course and other major UK universities are following suit. They may well begin by including practical PR as part of the communications studies aspect of degrees in business studies. Now, the ideal education and training is still held to embrace a degree in the arts or social sciences; a PPE (politics, philosophy and economics) or economics or sociology degree is regarded as an indicator of knowledge and analytical skills helpful in interpreting a rapidly changing political and socio-economic scene. A more vocationally guided course could well have appeal.

Meanwhile, more public relations consultancies are running their own training programmes. The CBI initiated training programmes for industry, particularly in the press relations area, which have been highly successful and very important. Other organisation are now running courses in communications, including the British Institute of Management. Large organisations like Barclays Bank and the larger financial institutions appreciate the importance of public relations and are allocating management time for the training function.

INCREASING PROFESSIONALISM

There is a rapidly growing awareness that public relations is no longer an amateur game. It is becoming increasingly specialist and sophisticated.

> Too many people tend to think that anybody can go and take a few journalists out to lunch, smile sweetly and pleasantly and entertain them and you get what you want. But it is not like that any more. There is much more research one needs to go into before you can actually project. Certainly this is so within the Civil Service.

Graduate recruitment has risen sharply, and public relations is now seen as a career prospect with professional respectability.

> Obviously there are characteristics which are common across all types of PR. But 'PR' really is such a generalisation. Product PR, for example, is so different from financial PR, or government PR, so you cannot really talk across the whole range.

> I have to admit there was a time when I would never admit to anybody that I was in PR. People used to get hostile, start dismissing one, which is so false, because of the sort of con-man image of PR.

But career progression is a problem in the PR industry. Most consultancies are small; in terms of organisation structure, they tend to be flat pyramids, with few layers, and hence limited opportunities for upward career progression through the hierarchy. Equally, there are few rungs up the promotion ladder in most in-house PR departments, the status of which very much depends on the view of PR taken by the organisation overall.

> That is very true within the Civil Service. Starting at the semi-clerical grade, going right up to the Chief Information Officer level, there are about six grades. There is always the argument in government that the person who is Information Officer is doing exactly the same as a Principal, and in fact possibly more. More of the work. Yet the grading system is rather cosmetic.

The criticism that too few well educated and well trained people are moving into public relations is still frequently made, but there is evidence of increasing professionalism and growing interest from people with professional career aspirations. The obvious remedy for offering rewarding career paths has now been widely recognised by the larger, publicly quoted, PR companies. However, there is still not enough planning for careers in the public relations industry as a whole.

> What tends to happen in the PR business is that people come to it late. Either that or you start off young; there is no sort of happy medium. People come to it late having been in some sort of semi-journalistic career, and think that PR might be rather nice. And they'll dabble, and they come in late. Or you get the raw person, who comes in lower down but does not have much of a ladder to move up. The only ladder seems to be starting your own company, as it were.

But there are signs that solutions are being worked out.

> I have had one university graduate here with an arts degree for the last year, and I have made a specific attempt to train him into the needs of this job. And a year has gone by and he has just done it! It has worked out rather well. But I must say it is very exhausting to do the job and to do the training. So I do not think I would want to spend another year training in the same detailed way, as I have done this time. But hopefully *he* can do it next time. I will then evaluate his success on his ability to train.

Job rotation is another exciting possibility.

> I have suggested, when the need has been apparent that we have someone else on the staff, that a line executive comes out of his job for a year, eighteen months or two years, spends the time here and then goes back. At the moment that has not been agreed to, but I think it will be in the future. It is normal in the States; they are much more flexible in their training.

HOW FEASIBLE IS FORMAL TRAINING?

Underlying all discussions on training in public relations is of course the fundamental question: to what extent can the necessary skills and abilities be acquired through any kind of formal programme?

> I do not think you can really. You could be taught how to write properly and how to take a scrappy brief and build it

up, and present it as a press release. Or enlarge it or expand it. By doing exercises. But you cannot really be taught more than the basic mechanics of *how* to do it.

In this respect, the stuff of public relations falls reasonably easily into two parts. First, there is a basic orientation towards other people; empathetic qualities are essential to the job. 'If you do not have that basic sort of orientation, you might as well not bother.'

Secondly, there is the craft aspect of the job; one draws a distinction between craft and art. And there clearly are aspects of the PR craft which can be taught. It is possible to teach that, through proper structuring and organising of the PR team, while one cannot eliminate 'half-past-five crises', the chances of their erupting can certainly be minimised. If, say, 90 per cent of activity is controlled, the system can probably accommodate 10 per cent of eruptions.

> I hope there is a degree of training but there will be experiences, a broad range of experiences, that with the training will make a PR person.

> As soon as you start training someone you are specialising . . . and losing the input that comes from those experiences. So that a nice combination of both would be nice. But on-the-job training and education really is the best possible thing for PR, I think.

Obviously, educational philosophies in a general sense will determine the nature and direction of training in public relations and broader attempts at management development. It seems plausible to suggest that real commitment to the role of PR is reflected in the level of resources allocated to the personal development of its staff.

> All of my section heads go to management training, to recognised management training courses. I am the only one that does not, because I reckon I have had mine outside and I really do not have the time. They all undergo this, and middle management, that is the senior information officers I have been talking about, they all undergo training too. The idea then is to gear them up to a point where they retain their professionalism, their specialism, but also manage their teams effectively.

I am a great believer in giving people their chance. An example: a clerk who became a successful film director, first within the industry but now with outside recognition. That is satisfying to me. In terms of formal training, we have a residential Staff College – the high fliers go there for six weeks of general management, broadening their knowledge of the industry, etc. We have a management development system in the Board, which is quite elaborate, and is taken quite seriously. Also I have arranged for people to swap jobs, either between the branches and Head Office or with other departments, the Department of Energy for instance. But only for a fortnight at a time; we agreed that was long enough. Evaluation of results? It is very useful for people working in London to see firsthand how branches operate.

But PR training and management development, as in the practice of PR itself, there is still the inevitable search to produce, even if only implicitly, proof of cost effectiveness.

It pays off, because we know who is good and who is bad, because we have got reports on them. More importantly, we feel there are some guys who have come up very well. Oh, extremely well, extremely well.

Well, it was useful. I did the old IPR exam many years ago, and it was good for me because it introduced me to whole areas which I was not working in at the time. I felt I was better as a result of it. I think, thinking about what you are doing and reading about what you are doing is never time wasted anyway. I think that the problem comes, perhaps, in other terms. How valuable is it, for example, for an engineer to go and do another further degree instead of spending two years actually working in the firm? It is a more difficult thing than PR where the number of courses available is fairly small and you do not take off too much time.

Appendix 1

Checklist of problem areas

Identified Problem Area	Action				
	Currently under discussion	Decision taken	Decision implemented	No action as yet	Shelved
1. *Corporate planning*					
1.1. Has the strategic decision yet been taken of whether either to stand still or to opt for continued development?					
1.2. What decisions have been discussed/taken re: the investment of some £00,000 profits? To what extent have the full possibilities been researched (eg acquisitions? consultancy? property bonds?)					
1.3. What is company policy on new business, ie are other directors being actively encouraged to pursue/develop new business opportunities?					

1.4. How are estimates reached of 'best' and 'worst' when planning for the organisation's future?

1.5. What rationale lay beneath the decision to seek a second account within the industry? How much research has been done into the industry's performance and future prospects?

1.6. Obvious problem area to have come out of recent appraisal/review document: why has there been a higher turnover but the same level of profit? The problems need to be well understood and communicated to all members of the organisation.

2. *Organisational development*

2.1. What decisions have been reached about the future development of the organisational structure of the company?

2.2. Specifically, what steps have been taken to ensure that it can most effectively receive prospective new business accounts?

Identified Problem Area	Action				
	Currently under discussion	*Decision taken*	*Decision implemented*	*No action as yet*	*Shelved*
How much thought has been expended on the process of getting new business, from the initial stage of searching for new business opportunities to the point where new business is incorporated into the organisational structure?					
2.3. How much improvement has there been over the past six-month period in lateral communications?					
2.4. What are the reasons for this? (a) less centralised control by the Chairman and Managing Director? (b) increased appreciation of the need for lateral communications? (c) conscious effort to make the necessary time despite high work pressure?					
2.5. What are the implications of this?					
2.6. Has a situation arisen where an ad hoc project coordinator has been appointed?					
2.7. What mechanisms/processes have been developed to foresee and to manage changes in the environment?					

2.8. Could it be said that the company has now moved successfully from the pioneering to the integrative stage of organisational development?

2.9. Is there now a greater 'sense of organisation' within the company?

2.10. What has been done to reduce the incidence of role conflict and ambiguity, and to make the effect of these conditions (when they cannot be avoided) minimally damaging to the person and to the organisation?

Which of these possibilities have been used?

(a) introduction of direct structural change;

(b) introduction of new criteria of selection and placement;

(c) increasing the tolerance and coping qualities of individuals;

(d) strengthening the interpersonal bonds among members of the organisation.

3. *Role of the Board and Management Group*

3.1. Have the roles and terms of reference of the Board and the Management Group now

Identified Problem Area	Action				
	Currently under discussion	Decision taken	Decision implemented	No action as yet	Shelved
been clearly defined, by some participative process?					
3.2 Have the following crucial relationships been clearly defined, by some participative process?					
(a) the relationship between the Board and the Management Group?					
(b) the relationship between the Board and the Chairman and Managing Director/principal shareholder?					
(c) the relationship between the Management Group and the other members of the organisation?					
3.3. Has there been any reduction in the ambiguity previously surrounding the role of Board Director?					
4. *Role of the Chairman and Managing Director*					
4.1. Have the two functions of *maintenance* (routine administrative work) and *adaptation* (the generation of new business and the formula-					

ticable, separated? Is the Chairman able to devote most of his or her energy to the second function, adaptation?

4.2. Has the *behaviour* of the Chairman and Managing Director changed to the extent that it now better fits the new *structure* of their role?

4.3. Has the Chairman yet decided whether he or she is to become Chairman or Chief Executive of the company?

5. *Role of the Chairman's deputy/No 2 person*

5.1. What decisions have been discussed/implemented about the role of the Chairman's deputy/No 2 person vis-à-vis

(a) the Chairman and Managing Director;

(b) the Directors of other groups;

(c) executives within Division A.

5.2. What efforts has he or she made toward the ordering of priorities vis-à-vis competing demands upon his or her time?

5.3. How has his or her allocation of time/priorities among the several aspects of his or her role changed over the past few months?

143

Identified Problem Area	Action				
	Currently under discussion	Decision taken	Decision implemented	No action as yet	Shelved
6. *Role of Y* What decisions have been discussed/implemented about the Role of Y?					
6.1. To what extent is it intended to develop Y?					
6.2. Is it considered that he or she will be promoted into his or her boss's current role, as and when he or she becomes Assistant Managing Director, ie effectively the No 2?					
7. *Recruitment of a new executive into Division A*					
7.1. By what processes have the new executive's role, role set and terms of reference been defined?					
7.2. What will be the relationship between the new executive and the Chairman? Will he or she have a direct reporting link to the No 2, and to the No 2 only?					
7.3. On which accounts will he or she be working?					
7.4. What steps will be taken to ensure that the currently existing '2-camp situation' is not perpetuated through this new recruit? The recruiting of a suitably qualified women					

for this role could do much to reduce the tension. (Currently all divisions run parallel, ie the
male/female divide reflects exactly the
Consumer Group/Industrial Group divide.)

7.5. The Chairman has said in discussion that the
big advantage of bringing in this new person
is that 'he /she will be purpose-built for the
job, so we can avoid any problems right from
the start.' What problems could be expected
to arise?

(a) Ambiguity re: roles of account directors,
account executives. This should be clar-
ified from the beginning. How will this
be done?

(b) Chairmans's involvement: would it be
preferable for the Chairman not to get
involved with the new executive's work,
but to rely completely on feedback
reports from his or her No 2?

7.6. The Chairman has said in discussion that he
or she will bear the initial costs of this new
executive, 'so that a wise decision may be
made from the organisation's point of view'.
Surely this will then be shown as an overhead, which will have to be borne in part by
all groups within the company? If so, how has
this been presented to the other directors?

Identified Problem Area	Action				
	Currently under discussion	Decision taken	Decision implemented	No action as yet	Shelved
8. *Role of staff personnel*					
8.1. What action has been taken to reduce the ambiguity in the roles of staff personnel?					
9. *Internal processes*					
9.1. In what ways have the internal control systems been improved during the last six-month period?					
9.2. Has there been any change in the level of morale within the company over the last six-month period? Have there been any visible indications that morale is either improving or weakening?					
What positive steps have been initiated in order to attempt to improve motivation?					
9.3. What efforts have been made to increase the levels of openness and trust within the company? Has any progress been made?					
9.4. What efforts have been made to improve the level of feedback to individuals about their work?					

146

Appendix 2

Checklist for evaluating and reviewing on-going relationships with clients

Potential problem area	Evaluation of current situation			Actual performance measured against budgeted forecasts		Action			
	Good	Satisfactory	Unsatisfactory	Actual	Budgeted	Currently under discussion	Decision taken	Decision implemented	No action as yet
1. *Time input*									
1.1. Client liaison									
● meetings									
● telephone									
● written									
1.2. Press liaison									
● preparing releases									
● selling releases									
● distributing releases									
● press conferences									
1.3. Special events (specify)									

147

Potential problem area	Evaluation of current situation			Actual performance measured against budgeted forecasts		Action			
	Good	Satisfactory	Unsatisfactory	Actual	Budgeted	Currently under discussion	Decision taken	Decision implemented	No action as yet
1.4. Planning									
1.5. Reporting									
1.6. Miscellaneous									
2. Costs									
2.1. Fixed costs									
2.2. Variable costs									
3. Role definition									
3.1. Is there any ambiguity in the definition of the specialist's role?									
3.2. Is there any conflict in the definition of the specialist's role?									
3.3. Is there clear communication of									

role expectations between specialists and the client?

3.4. Has the specialist's role developed in any way since the beginning of the relationship?

4. *Campaign effectiveness*

4.1. Have campaigns mounted for the client been successful? Why?

4.2. What results have the campaigns(s) achieved?

5. *Evaluation of creative input*

5.1. What level of innovation has gone into the campaign(s)?

Potential problem area	Evaluation of current situation			Actual performance measured against budgeted forecasts		Action			
	Good	Satisfactory	Unsatisfactory	Actual	Budgeted	Currently under discussion	Decision taken	Decision implemented	No action as yet
5.2. To what extent has the campaign(s) been characterised by 'new' activities/ideas?									
6. Implementation									
6.1. Has the campaign(s) been well organised? What criticisms could be made?									
6.2. Have resources been used in an optimal way?									
6.3. Was the planning of the campaign satisfactory? Eg have any problems/panics/omissions arisen which									

_____

_____

_____

_____

_____

_____

_____

could have perhaps
been avoided with
more careful planning?

6.4. Has there been good
cooperation with the
client?

6.5. Has there been good
cooperation with the
press?

6.6. Has the campaign
been well integrated

(a) so as to provide a
coherent 'plan of
attack'?

(b) within the
specialist
department/cons-
ultancy?

(c) with the activities
of the client
organisation?

(d) with the press?

(e) with other

Potential problem area	Evaluation of current situation			Actual performance measured against budgeted forecasts		Action			
	Good	Satisfactory	Unsatisfactory	Actual	Budgeted	Currently under discussion	Decision taken	Decision implemented	No action as yet
external organisations, eg advertising agencies?									
7. *Is the approach proactive?* Has the approach been proactive rather than reactive? Does the specialist department/consultancy take the initiative vis-à-vis making contact with: (a) the client? (b) the press? (c) other external organisations, eg the public etc?									

8. *Communication*

8.1. Is the message being communicated?

8.2. Is the message being communicated to the right people?

8.3. Is the message being received?

How can this be proven?

8.4. What is happening *as a result* of that message being communicated and received?

9. *Optimal use of resources*

Are resources being used effectively according to the following formula: given the *process* of the PR activity, is the *output* satisfactory vis-à-vis the *input*? Eg are

Potential problem area	Evaluation of current situation			Actual performance measured against budgeted forecasts		Action			
	Good	Satisfactory	Unsatisfactory	Actual	Budgeted	Currently under discussion	Decision taken	Decision implemented	No action as yet
the right staff being used for the right jobs?									
10. Summary									
Has the campaign to date been effective from the point of view of the specialist?									
10.1. Have there so far been any indications of latent dissatisfaction from the client?									
10.2. What are the prospects for renewal of the account?									
10.3. Is the account currently profitable?									

Appendix 3

Subjective questionnaire for use in evaluating and reviewing on-going relationships with clients

These questions are intentionally open-ended and non-directive, so as to elicit as far as possible the client's precise feelings. Examples should be encouraged wherever possible, for example: 'Well, I thought the consultancy should really have done X, Y and Z without our having to ask them.'

1. In which areas are you most satisfied with your present relationship with the consultancy?

2. In which areas are you least satisfied with your present relationship with the consultancy?

3. Are there any of the consultancy's activities which you would like it to do differently?

4. Would you like the consultancy to do anything else which it does not do now?

5. Would you prefer the consultancy *not* to do something which it does now?

6. How would you try to alter the consultancy's behaviour to fit your own expectations/preferences better?

7. Do you think that the consultancy is clear about your own level of satisfaction with the present campaign(s)?

8. Does the consultancy usually make itself clear when it wants or expects something from you?

9. Do you think the consultancy is clear about your own expectations of their involvement in your organisation?

Appendix 4

Specimen activity record

Name.. Date...............

Activity number	Client	Type of activity								Other people involved			Initiation		Channel			Regularity			Time (minutes)		
		Client liaison	Press release	Press conference	Special event	Planning	Reporting	Miscellaneous		Own staff	Client	External	Initiated by self	Initiated by client	Meeting	Telephone	Written	Regular	Ad hoc	Interruption	0–5	5–30	30+
1																							
2																							
3																							
4																							

Appendix 4

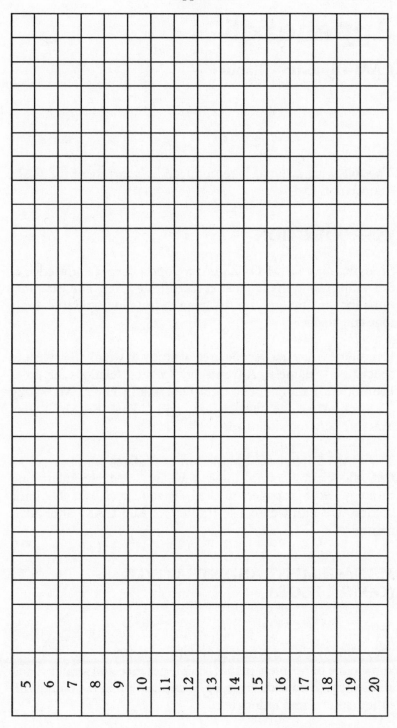

157

Appendix 5

CAM Diploma syllabus

The following syllabus is reproduced by courtesy of the CAM Foundation Ltd.

INTRODUCTION

Studying for a CAM Diploma develops a deeper knowledge of the subject than that gained at Certificate level. The examinations for the Diploma are designed to test your ability to apply that knowledge.

Candidates may choose the area of study in which they wish to specialise – namely, Advertising, Public Relations or Sales Promotion. Examinations for a Diploma in Direct Marketing are conducted in association with The British Direct Marketing Association Ltd.

The CAM Diploma is awarded to candidates who have satisfied the examiners in three subjects – Management and Strategy *plus* two papers in their chosen specialism. Diploma holders are entitled to use the letters Dip CAM after their name.

MANAGEMENT AND STRATEGY (COMPULSORY)

Aim

The aim of this module is to give candidates an in-depth knowledge of business management, practice and strategy, and allow them to consider its specific application in the communication and related industries.

On completion of this module candidates will have a knowledge of the organisation and structure of all types of enterprises, the financing of them and management procedures and practice. They will also be able to analyse situations, develop the appropriate strategies in pursuance of organisational objectives and be able to apply the practice of management to the communication industry.

Objectives

On completion of this module candidates should know how:

- To describe and examine the different forms of organisational structure
- To examine the sources of finance available to organisations
- To examine the process of management at corporate and business unit level
- To analyse situations and develop appropriate strategies consistent with corporate goals
- To describe the functions, duties and techniques of management
- To develop management skills for all types of organisations, commercial and non-commercial
- To apply the above to the communication and related industries.

1. Organisational structures

- Single-owner firms, partnerships and co-partnerships
- Public and private companies, interlocking and holding companies, amalgamation, mergers, monopolies and cartels
- Cooperative undertakings
- Professional institutions and trade associations
- Central and local government, public bodies, charities and membership organisations
- Alternative corporate structures: matrix, pyramid etc.
- Line and staff management
- Entrepreneurs and Intrapreneurs
- Global, multi-national, international.

2. Financing of organisations

- Sources of capital, internal and external
- Financing of enterprises
- Capital market: domestic and international
- Venture capital
- Government and private subsidies and grants.

3. Management–the planning process

This section covers the process of planning including situation analysis, strategy option generation, implementation and implications for the communication and marketing mix.

- Organisational objectives – corporate, strategic, tactical
- Defining the business
- The strategic Audit – Strengths, Weaknesses. Opportunities and Threats (SWOT)
- Integration of objectives: corporate, institutional, business, marketing operational, communications and other functional
- Portfolio analysis/use of matrices:
  —Boston Consulting Group Matrix
  —Market Growth (brand share)
  —Market attractiveness
  —Market maturity/competitive strength
- Profit Impact of Marketing Strategy
- Creative approaches, eg Porter, organic, changing rules of the competitive game
- Resource allocation
- Competitive analysis – Product life cycles and Experience Curve effects
- Audience segmentation/target market opportunities
- Corporate and product positioning/brand mapping
- Uses of primary and secondary market/marketing research
- Search for profit in declining markets
- Legal/voluntary/ethical constraints
- Implementation: marketing mix planning, sources of competitive advantage, the role of communication in achieving strategic goals.

4. Management – practice

- Management functions, techniques, duties and responsibilities
- Managing personnel, change, conflict and developments in organisations, the importance of interpersonal skills and interface skills/relationship within and between organisations' departments
- Planning, control and evaluating performance/resources including human resources
  - —performance criteria, control and evaluation
  - —forecasting, budgetary, costing and statistical controls
  - —financial analysis – DFC, cashflow, break even
  - —human resource analyses, recruitment procedures, control, evaluation
  - —uses of marketing audit, marketing and audience research and operational research techniques
  - —awareness of legal/voluntary/ethical constraints, eg Trades Union Legislation.

5. Management – communication industry applications

- The role of in-house and external services and their inter-relationships
- Management, organisation and structure of Advertising Agencies, Media Independents, PR and PR consultancies, Sales Promotion Houses, Direct Marketing, Market Research Agencies etc
- Specific management problem areas in the above.

Reading list

Essential reading

Organisation
John Child; Paul Chapman
Organisational Theory
Bryan & Cronin; Mitchell Beazley

Supplementary reading

Marketing: Planning, Analysis and Control
P Kotler; Prentice Hall
Competitive Strategy

M E Porter; Macmillan
Understanding Organisations
C Handy; Penguin

Other reading

Market Research for Managers
S Crouch; Heinemann
Practice of Management
P Drucker; Heinemann
Economics
F Livesey; Heinemann
Management
H Koontz, C O'Donnell and H Wiehrich; McGraw Hill

PUBLIC RELATIONS MANAGEMENT

Introduction

Public relations is a function or task of management which presents a particular set of demands to those having responsibility for managing the function and integrating it effectively into the overall management of an organisation.

This paper requires an understanding of the principles of public relations management in organisations in the public, private, non-profit and other sectors, and of public relations programme management in consultancy settings.

Aim

The syllabus for this paper is designed to provide a basis for assessing the candidate's knowledge of principles of public relations management, their application to public relations programme development and activities in organisations, and their application in the integration of public relations into overall management planning and decision making.

Objectives

On completion of this module candidates should be able:

- To describe and examine public relations as a function and/or task of management in and for organisations in the

162

public, private, non-profit and other sectors. Organisations in each of those sectors include the following.

Public sector

—Government and government agencies – national, local and international
—Quangos: quasi autonomous non-governmental organisations
—Public utilities
—Education bodies, authorities; trusts
—Broadcasting authorities.

Private sector

—Corporations
—Business organisations
—Professional partnerships
—Financial institutions.

Non-profit

—Charities

—Community, youth and voluntary organisations
—Other organisations; membership associations
—Professional bodies
—Trade associations
—Campaigning organisations – pressure and minority interest groups
—Religious groups and organisations
—Political parties
—Trade unions.

- To examine the opportunities and constraints for public relations management presented by organisations in each of these sectors, whether the public relations resource is internal, external, or a combination of the two.
- To examine public relations' contribution to overall management planning and decision making, to financial, personnel and marketing management, and to internal communication, employee relations and organisational development.
- To examine candidates' knowledge of other organisation

163

and key publics and their likely impact on the organisations and its public relations activities, for example government agencies or local, national and international levels including the EC, other regulatory bodies, the Charities Commission, the media, special interest groups and the local community.

- To examine knowledge of specific topics in public relations management including:
  —The use of research, auditing, scanning and monitoring techniques in issues management, programme and evaluation
  —Strategic planning
  —Planning processes and techniques
  —Communications programme planning, budgeting and implementation
  —Crisis management and crisis communication
  —Issues management
  —Legal issues
  —Staffing public relations positions
  —Structuring and managing the public relations department
  —Managing external services and creative staff
  —Public relations programme management in consultancy settings
  —The role of the public relations practitioner as a consultant and phases in the consultation process
  —Establishing the way to balance the use of internal and external resources to the best effect.

Reading list

See page 166.

PUBLIC RELATIONS PRACTICE

Introduction

Public relations management depends on knowledge of, and skill in applying, a number of techniques drawn from general management and from public relations practice.

This paper will seek to show, on a case study basis, that candidates understand how the techniques of public relations management are applied within organisations, in public, private and non-profit sectors, and in consultancy settings

Aim

This paper is intended to test candidates' ability to apply in practice the principles and techniques of public relations and public relations management to problems and opportunities faced by organisations.

Objectives

- To provide opportunities, through the use of case studies, for candidates to demonstrate that they understand how the principles and techniques of public relations and public relations management may be applied to the exploitation of opportunities and to the solution of problems faced in practice

- To test candidates' knowledge of commercial, marketing, city and financial applications.

- To test candidates knowledge of the application, in the case studies presented, of consulting techniques and specific techniques such as:

  —Social, market and communication research techniques

  —Trend analysis

  —Management by objectives, programme evaluation and review techniques (PERT), and critical path methods of programme planning

  —Strategic planning

  —Programme budgeting

  —Communication programme planning, budgeting and implementation.

- To test candidates' abilities to make decisions regarding approaches to staff selection, personnel and project management, delegation of tasks and control of activities.
- To examine candidates' knowledge of the use and effectiveness of currently available communications tech-

niques, including those depending on the use of communication technology.

Case study practice

Students should keep abreast of current news items and regularly read the financial and political pages of the press. Case studies are likely to be related to current events.

Reading list

Candidates sitting the PR Diploma papers are advised to read as widely as possible. The following books are of value in developing an in-depth knowledge of the subjects.

Company Image and Reality
David Bernstein; Holt, Rinehart & Winston
Doing Business in the European Community
John Drew; Butterworth
Local Government for Journalists
Geoffrey Smith; LGC Communications
McNae's Essential Law for Journalists
ed Walter Greenwood & Tom Welsh; Butterworth
Managing Corporate Relations
George S Moore; Gower Press
The Media in Britain
Jeremy Tunstall; Constable
Planned Press and Public Relations
Frank Jefkins; Blackie
Public Relations is Your Business
Colin Coulson-Thomas; Business Books
Successful Media Relations: A Practitioner's Guide
Judith Ridgeway; Gower
The Practice of Public Relations
Wilfred Howard; Heinemann
All about PR
Roger Haywood; McGraw Hill
Public Relations – A Practical Guide
C Coulson-Thomas; Pitman
This PR Consultancy Business
N Mendes; Mendes 1984
Financial Marketing and Communications

Kain Newman; Holt, Rinehart & Winston
Effective Public Relations
S Cutlip, A Center & G Broom; Prentice Hall
Managing Public Relations
J Grunig & T Hunt; Holt, Rinehart & Winston
Manual of Public Relations
Bowman & Ellis; Heinemann

CONSUMER ADVERTISING

Aim

Candidates are expected to show a grasp of the general application of advertising (and other forms of marketing communication) to the overall marketing framework. This is, above all,
a communication examination with the emphasis on communication within the marketing mix, rather than on marketing in
total. Candidates must demonstrate a knowledge of the marketing environment into which communication will fit: they
will also be expected to show that they are current in terms of
practice.

Objectives

On completion of this module candidates will:

- Have an understanding of the elements of marketing com-
munication planning
- Be able to examine the elements of the Marketing
Communication plan, the media and research for evalua-
tion of the plan
- Have a knowledge of the organisation for advertising
- Have illustrations of the above with concrete samples.

1. General

- The role of publicity and communication within an overall
marketing programme

- The establishment of precise advertising, publicity and
promotion objectives

- The development of advertising strategies.

2. Campaign planning

● The evaluation of communication problems and the coordinated use of all available advertising methods, both media and creative, for problem solving. In particular, the steps needed to construct a total communication programme.

3. Budgeting

● The establishment of budgets for consumer communication programmes

4. The promotional mix

● The inter-relation of above-the-line and below-the-line techniques. How promotion may be built into marketing and communication strategies.

5. Research and evaluation

● The use of research within a communication programme. Tracking Studies. How to evaluate the elements of an advertising and promotional plan.

6. Organisation

● Organisation for advertising
● Agency/client relationship
● Types of advertising structure within companies.

Reading list

Essential reading

Complete Guide to advertising
Douglas; Macmillan
Advertising: What it is and how to do it
White; McGraw-Hill

Supplementary reading

Advertising Works (Vols I & II)
Broadbent; Hall Saunders
Advertising Works (Vols III & IV)
Channon; Cassell

20 Advertising Case Histories
IPA; Cassell

Other Reading

Marketing Management

Kotler; Prentice Hall

BUSINESS TO BUSINESS ADVERTISING

Aim

To show the practice of industrial marketing and advertising, with emphasis on the planning of integrated campaigns. The way the industrial marketing operation is organised in companies, and the methods of obtaining facts about the market place. The different types of communication channels and the data available to assess them. The place of public relations in industrial marketing, and the relations with other industrial communications.

Objectives

On completion of this module candidates will:

- Have a knowledge of the role of communication in the context of the Industrial Marketing Communication campaign
- Be able to examine the steps involved in designing an Industrial Marketing Communication campaign
- Be able to describe and examine the role of Research, Media and Public Relations as part of the Industrial Communications campaign
- Be able to describe the role of supplier organisations.

1. General

- The role of communication in the context of the industrial marketing plan
- The differences between industrial (or business-to-business) and consumer purchasing, and the variations in pur-

169

chasing patterns, the decision making unit and buying influences within industry for different types of product

- The importance of setting clear precise communication objectives from which integrated, multi-media campaigns are planned for product, service or corporate advertising
- How much should be spent: methods of determining budgets based on up-to-date knowledge of costs and appreciation of the size of budgets normally required to promote industrial goods
- Measuring the results and cost effectiveness of different types of communication activity
- Legal and voluntary restraints which must be considered when planning an industrial campaign.

2. Company organisation

- Types of marketing and publicity structures within industrial companies: identifying buying influences and their relative importance for different types of products and methods of distribution
- The role of the sales force and the contribution made by distributors or sales agents in communication.

3. Research

- Industrial marketing research: sources of information and techniques for desk research
- Application of the Standard Industrial Classification (SIC) system
- Evaluation of sales and measuring advertising effectiveness.

4. Media

- The strengths and weaknesses of *all* types of media for industrial advertising: press (newspapers, weekly periodicals, magazines, trade and technical and professional journals); literature; direct mail; exhibitions; films; television; radio; outdoor advertising; telephone selling; point of sale and audio-visual material
- A broad knowledge of current levels of costing in each of these areas.

5. Media research

- Qualitative and quantitative methods of assessing reader-ship and circulation
- The Industrial Media Data Form (MDF) and the Exhibition Data Form (EDF)
- The limitations of standard research reports as a guide to media selection
- Data specifically prepared for industrial use.

6. Public relations

- The role of PR in business-to business communications

7. Supplier organisations

- Advertising agencies–contracts and agreements
- Exhibition organisers and contractors
- Direct mail agents
- Sales promotion consultancies
- Printers.

Reading list

Essential reading

Practical Advertising and Publicity
Norman Hart; McGraw-Hill
The Fundamentals of Advertising
John Wilmshurst; Heinemann

Supplementary reading

Guide to Industrial Publicity ISBA
Industrial Marketing Digest, Reed Publishing
Business Marketing (monthly), Crain Communications, USA

Other reading

Guide for Exhibitors, ISBA
Guide to Direct Mail Advertising, ISBA
The Marketing of Industrial Products
Norman Hart; McGraw-Hill
How to Succeed in Advertising, IPA

Effective Conferences and Meetings
David Seeking; Kogan Page

INTERNATIONAL ADVERTISING

Introduction

The course is designed to examine variations in marketing and advertising practice when applied in more than one country.

Primary emphasis is placed on advertising and marketing in the countries of your own region so that the lessons learned can be developed in some depth. But the underlying objective of the course is to extend principles to global marketing considerations.

Aims

The aim is for candidates to learn how to succeed in marketing and advertising products and services internationally covering the organisation and all sales facets. Part of the course is necessarily devoted to gaining knowledge, but candidates should also understand its practical applications and will be examined on this in the form of a case study.

Objectives

On completion of this module candidates should know:

- How to approach international markets and how to decide which or what market
- How first to enter a market and how to react within an established market from both an organisational and marketing stand point, understanding the country-by-country and the pan-country international approach
- The importance and implications of global organisation and marketing
- How to assess and create a plan for marketing internationally with realistic goals and budgets which can be justified.

1. International marketing background

Strategy and Organisation for Marketing Abroad.

- How to develop into an overseas market
- Principal factors determining market organisation, product market, company structure
- Types of structure – sales agent, export sales department, offices abroad; advantages/disadvantages of global organisation
- International Marketing Planning – market differences, product pricing, sales support, cost, profit
- Methods of handling promotion overseas.

2. Market characteristics

- Basic economic advertising facts about countries in your region; industry, language, media available, limitations on products and sales activities, competition.

3. Intelligence for marketing abroad

- Categories of information required/available
- Sources and uses of information
- Practical limitations
- Sources of desk research
- Special applications for international marketing
- Special techniques
- Size of markets and their demographics.

4. International communication practice

- Communication Strategy and Coordination
- Appropriate degrees of coordination
- Advantages
- The coordinator's role in, and outside, the marketing company.

5. Research for international advertising

- Special problems overseas, comparison, pan-frontier
- Sources
- Techniques
- Measuring effectiveness.

6. Advertising agency organisation

- Types of agency structure
- Relationship with client structure
- Problems of exclusivity
- Remuneration
- Agency/client contracts.

7. Advertising media

- Characteristics and knowledge of international media and the main individual country media – press, TV, outdoor, direct mail
- Media buying practice
- Media data.

8. Media research

- Availability/Usage

- Knowledge of the major national and international media researches.

9. Creating the plan

- Budgeting
- Control
- Assessment
- Understanding the need and how to plan forward over a number of years
- Extending the plan forward to enable assessment of expenditure, potential market share, success, profit, market and organisational development.

10. Advertising creative

- Methods of producing overseas advertising
- Quality control
- Translation
- Local regulations affecting advertising
- Creativity across borders.

Appendix 5

Reading list

Essential reading

Case Studies in International Marketing P Doyle & N A Hart;
Heinemann
International Marketing
Stanley J Paliwoda; Heinemann

Supplementary reading

International Marketing

L S Walsh; (M E Handbook) Pitman
Competition in Global Industries Ed Michael Porter; Harvard
Business School Press
Competitive Advantage Michael Porter; Free Press (New York)
Media International (monthly) 27 Wilfred Street, London SW1E
6PR

SALES PROMOTION MANAGEMENT AND STRUCTURE

Aim

To provide candidates with an in-depth knowledge of the
management and structure of Sales Promotion and its practical
application.

Objectives

On completion of this module candidates will have:

- an understanding of the management and structure of
  Sales Promotion
- knowledge on how to devise a Sales Promotion campaign
- an understanding of the role of Sales Promotion agencies,
  promotion, distribution companies, the trade and fulfilment houses
- an understanding of the Administration and controls
  affecting a Sales Promotion campaign
- a practical understanding of how to apply Sales Promotion
  campaigns and techniques.

175

1. **The management structure of Sales Promotion**

- The Management of Sales Promotion
- Strategic promotional planning within the marketing planning process
- the role of Sales Promotion compared to other marketing elements
- The different role of Sales Promotion in packaged goods compared to durables, Service compared to Retail Industries
- Sales Promotions and the brand manager
- 'in house' promotion activities
- The role of the client.

2. **Elements of a Sales Promotion campaign**

- Definition and quantification of promotional objectives
- Selection of Promotional Strategy
- Factors affecting Promotional Strategy
- Selection of technique according to budget, legal or other constraints
- Design of the promotional elements
- Promotion execution, timing and administration
- Promotional evaluation – its importance and methods
- Target Audience definition
- Differentiation between promotional techniques
- Estimation of Agency fees
- Tax and VAT implications of Free Offers and Incentives
- Salesforce and other incentives
- 'Postage and Packaging' type offers
- Estimation of Artwork, POS, Incentive, Mail Out, handling and other costs.

3. **Sales Promotion facilitators**

- Historical perspective
- Different types of agencies
- International Sales Promotion Agencies
- Criteria for selection
- Methods of remuneration
- Briefing
- Organisation

- Distribution techniques
- Control, monitoring and evaluation
- Definition of the various types, advantages, disadvantages and factors affecting redemption, adminstration
- Advertorial promotions
- Banded Offers
- Buyback/Refund offers
- Selection of Fulfilment Houses
- Types of Fulfilment Houses
- Adminstration and reporting procedures
- Considerations with licensed products
- Complaints procedure, monitoring and evaluation
- Refund of money
- Handling procedures for the replacement of faulty or damaged premiums.

4. **Administration, statutory and self regulatory controls**

- The British Code of Sales Promotion Practice
- The Role of the Code of Advertising Practice Committee and Advertising Standards Authority
- The Role of The Institute of Sales Promotion
- The EEC and Sales Promotion.

Reading list

See page 181.

SALES PROMOTION PRACTICE

Aim

To provide candidates with an in-depth knowledge of Sales Promotion techniques and their practical application.

Objectives

On completion of this module candidates will have:

- an understanding of the role of Sales Promotion techniques and terminology

177

- a knowledge of how research can help in the development of Sales Promotion devices
- an understanding of the different types of Sales Promotion, their use, advantages and disadvantages
- an understanding of the statutory and self-regulatory controls concerning Sales Promotion techniques
- a practical understanding of how to apply Sales Promotion techniques.

1. The role of Sales Promotion techniques and Sales Promotion terminology

- The effect of Promotions on Brands
- Appreciation of Promotional terms
- The different role of Sales Promotion in packaged goods compared to durables, Service compared to Retail Industries.

2. The role of research

- Use of Market Research in setting promotional targets
- Testing promotional ideas
- Measuring consumer attitudes to promotions
- Screening tests and Consumer surveys
- Monitoring competitive activity
- Use of Continuous Market Research Data (AGB, ACORN, etc).

3. Sales Promotion techniques

The role, advantages and disadvantages of:

Promotional techniques

- Definition of the various types, advantages, disadvantages and factors affecting redemption, administration
- Advertorial promotions
- Banded Offers
- Buyback/Refund Offers
- Charity Promotions
- Competitions
- Coupons (Money off)
- Direct Mail

- Door to Door Leaflets
- Free Draws and Sweepstakes
- Free In-Pack, On-Pack and With-Pack Offers
- Free Mail Ins
- Free Product Offers
- Multibrand promotions
- Personality promotions
- Reusable Container Premiums
- Sampling
- Self Liquidating Premiums
- Shareouts/Giveaways
- Tailormade Promotions
- Trading Stamps.

Promotional items and premiums

- Types of Premiums
- Executive Gifts as promotional tools
- Criteria for selection
- Suitability
- Quality
- Description
- Specification
- Supply.

Coupons

- Relative merits of couponing versus money off
- Handling allowances
- Trade redemption channels
- Types of coupons
- Retailer (store specific) coupon promotions
- In-and On-pack coupons
- Advantages of coupons by distribution method
- Cross couponing
- Redemption, timing and phasing of financial liability
- Coupon distribution and redemption by media, manufacturer/retailer split
- Misredemption and Malredemption
- Controls on coupon promotions
- The Nielsen Clearing House
- Coupon promotion costs
- Trends in couponing.

Redemption

- Factors affecting response rate
- Methods of estimating.

Selling in

- Methods of stimulating manufacturers, wholesalers and retailers sales forces
- Trade deals and Allowances
- Merchandise and Cost Incentives
- Travel Incentives
- Dealer and Sales Force Incentive programmes; developing a budget, different types of Awards
- Trade shows and exhibitions.

Point of purchase (POP)

- Historical perspective
- Scope of POP advertising today
- Advantages and disadvantages of POP advertising
- Types of POP advertising
- Constraints eg retailer
- How POP advertising relates to other media
- Retailers attitudes to POP advertising.

Implications of new technology

- Electronic Point of Sale
- Holography
- Individual serialisation of coupons.

Promotional communication

- Media available and their relative merits
- Services available to assist promoters
- Security aspects of promotion eg scratchcards.

4. Statutory and self-regulatory controls

- Main laws affecting promotions
- Mail Order Protection Scheme
- Mailing Preference Service
- Royalty, Bank of England constraints

- Children and Promotions
- Limitations to Promotional Offers eg Country of origin marking
- Promotions on hazardous products
- Prohibited promotional techniques eg with medicinal products
- Proof of purchase considerations, criteria for selection.

Reading list

Essential reading

The Manual of Sales promotion
J Williams; Innovation Ltd
The British Code of Sales Promotion Practice: Managing Sales Promotion
J Piper; Gower Press 1980

Supplementary reading

Choosing the Right Sales Promotion
A Toop; The Sales Machine, London
The Creative Element in Sales Promotion
A Toop; The Sales Machine

A Wolfe; Research studies sponsored by the Institute of Sales Promotion
i) 'Promotion Sales: What motivates the retailer and consumer'
ii) 'Sales Promotion Tomorrow's World' 1983

Other reading

How British Industry Promotes
S Gentry & L Rodger; Industrial Marketing Research Ltd 1977
Promotional Marketing
E Adler; Headline Promotions 1977
Guide to Sales Promotion
J Ward; Institute of Practitioners in Advertising 1977

Direct marketing

Candidates for a CAM Diploma in Direct Marketing are required to take the (compulsory) Management & Strategy paper *plus* the BDMA Diploma examination

Details of the BDMA examinations may be obtained from:

The Direct Marketing Centre
Millennium House
21 Eden Walk
Kingston-upon-Thames
Surrey KT1 1BL

Appendix 6
Public Relations
Education*

SEMINARS AND SHORT PUBLIC RELATIONS COURSES

1. Public Relations Consultants Association – Tel: 071-233 6026
2. British Association of Industrial Editors – Tel:0732 459331
3. CIM Marketing Training Seminars – Tel: 0628 524922/2229
4. Industrial Society (communications skills dept) – Tel: 071-839 4300
5. Interact International Ltd – Tel: 0892 515222
6. Royal Institute of Public Adminstration – Tel: 071-222 2248
7. Trident Training Services – tailormade short courses – Tel: 081-874 3610
8. Henshall Centre, Stockport – Tel: 061-440 8466

DEGREE COURSES (Bachelor and Masters)

1. University of Stirling. MSc in Public Relations. One year full-time. Tel: 0786 73171
2. Bournemouth University. BA (Hons) in Public Relations. Four years full-time. Tel: 0202 524111
3. College of St Mark and St John, Plymouth (part of the University of Exeter). BA (Hons) in Public Relations. Three years full-time. Tel: 0752 777188

*This appendix is reproduced with the kind permission of the Institute of Public Relations.

4. Leeds Polytechnic, Business School. BA (Hons) in Public Relations.
   Three years full-time Tel: 0532 832600
5. Cranfield School of Management. MBA.
   Two years part time or one year full-time, with public relations, public affairs and corporate communications elective. Tel: 0234 751122 ext 3184
6. Napier University. BA in Communication.
   Three years full-time. Tel: 031-444 2266

CERTIFICATE AND DIPLOMA COURSES

1. CAM Certificate and Diploma. Courses are available at many colleges throughout Britain, part-time, full-time and distance learning. Tel: 071-828 7506
2. West Herts College. Post-graduate Diploma in International Public relations. One year full-time. Tel: 0923 257500
3. Frank Jefkins School of Communication. London Chamber of Commerce and Industry Group Diploma and CAM Certificate and Diploma (Distance learning) – Tel: 0689 847282
4. Cathy Ace & Associates. CAM Certificate and Diploma (Distance Learning/Intensive Study Weekends). Tel: 081-671 0584

PUBLIC RELATIONS EDUCATION AND TRAINING MATRIX

This document sets out the broad range of knowledge and skills necessary to a Public Relations professional. It has been developed with and endorsed by The Institute of Public Relations and the Public Relations Consultants Association. It is designed as a basis for:

- self-assessment of training needs and career development
- appraisal of employees' skills and their development needs

● evaluation of training and education course suitability.

THE MATRIX

The matrix is in four categories:

A: Knowledge
B: Writing Skills
C: Public Relations Skills
D: Business Skills.

Five stages of knowledge, skills or experience have been identified:

Stage 1 **pre-entry requirements** – basic skills and knowledge necessary for any candidate wishing to pursue a
career in public relations – these may be obtained
while working in an administrative role

Stage 2 **professional starter** – specific initial knowledge
and skills essential for those developing their public
relations career, from assistants and junior executives

**Stages 3
and 4** **developing and operating professional** – development, knowledge and skills, necessarily gained
over a period of time, to become a fully rounded and
experienced public relations practitioner and public
relations operator

Stage 5 **experienced professional specialist and management** – the continuing development phase from
functional to team or group supervision responsibility, counselling and management roles in public
relations.

PUBLIC RELATIONS INDUSTRY TRAINING GUIDE

		KNOWLEDGE	Stage:	1	2	3	4	5
A	1	The Role of Public Relations, both in-house and consultancy, in commercial and public sector organisations.		X	X	X	X	X
	2	An appreciation of the range of techniques and media available to public relations practitioners in the UK.		X	X	X	X	X
	3	The role, responsibilities, value systems and reporting structures of the public relations function both inside the organisation and with outside bodies such as the Press, clients, local and national government and the Trades Unions.			X	X	X	X
	4	The role, responsibilities, vocabulary, techniques law and regulations of:						
		public relations;			X	X	X	X
		marketing;			X	X	-	-
		advertising;			X	X	-	-
		research and behavioural studies; and production of printed media.			X	X	X	X
	5	The role, responsibilities, vocabulary, techniques, ethics, law and regulations of:						
		sponsorship;			X	X	-	-
		sales promotion;			X	X	-	-
		direct marketing; and			X	X	-	-
		broadcasting.			X	X	X	X
	6	The structure, priorities, distribution, basic economics, organisation, and operation of:						
		manufacturing industry;			X	X	X	X
		service industry;			X	X	X	X
		financial institutions;			X	X	X	X
		the public sector;			X	X	X	X
		local and national government;			X	X	X	X
		voluntary organisations;			X	X	X	X
		member organisations.			X	X	X	X
	7	Organisational strategy and policy making, both concept and practice.					X	X
	8	The legal, legislative and regulatory framework of Britain and the EEC.		X	X	X	X	X
	9	Managerial psychology:						
		motivation;					X	X
		leadership.					X	X
		WRITING SKILLS						
B	1	Business writing: agenda		X	X	X	X	X
	2	meeting notes		X	X	X	X	X
	3	memoranda		X	X	X	X	X
	4	letters		X	X	X	X	X
	5	Business writing: reports: proposals		X	X	X	X	X
		Business writing: reports: planning						
		Business writing: reports: progress		X	X	X	X	X
	6	Editorial writing: photocalls						
		interview calls			X	X	X	X
	8	news releases			X	X	X	X
	9	photo captions			X	X	X	X

PUBLIC RELATIONS INDUSTRY TRAINING GUIDE

		WRITING SKILLS CONTD. Stage	1	2	3	4	5
	10	briefing material		X	X	X	X
	11	feature material		X	X	X	X
	12	newsletters		X	X	X	X
	13	Presentation writing: script planning		X	X	X	X
	14	script writing		X	X	X	X
		PUBLIC RELATIONS SKILLS					
C	1	Understanding Public Relations objectives and strategies.		X	X	X	X
	2	Identifying Publics.		X	X	X	X
	3	Selecting Media to reach identified publics.		X	X	X	X
	4	Compiling contact lists.	X	X	X	X	X
	5	Media liaison techniques and operation.		X	X	X	X
	6	Understanding the differing emphasis of different market sectors, such as: consumer; technical; and financial.		X X X	X X X	X X X	X X X
	7	Editorial planning and monitoring.		X	X	X	X
	8	Handling editorial enquiries.		X	X	X	X
	9	The basics of photography.		X	X	X	X
	10	Briefing a photographer.		X	X	X	X
	11	Event planning and organisation.		X	X	X	X
	11a	Sponsorship selection, planning and organisation.		X	X	X	X
	12	Editorial promotions (competitions, special offer advertising).		X	X	X	X
	13	Negotiating editorial features and interviews.		X	X	X	X
	14	Briefing designers.		X	X	X	X
	15	Print selection, briefing and production management.		X	X	X	X
	16	Audio/visual briefing and production management.		X	X	X	X
	17	Exhibition planning and management.		X	X	X	X
	18	Capabilities of desktop publishing.		X	X	X	X
	19	Reviewing and implementing emergency plans.		X	X	X	X
	20	Understanding the implications of international developments in the media.			X	X	X
C	21	Formulating Public Relations Objectives.			X	X	X
	22	Developing Public Relations strategies – overall			X	X	X
	23	– contingency				X	X
	24	Creating Public Relations plans for action.			X	X	X
	25	Identifying trends, risks and issues relevant to an organisation.			X	X	X
	26	Monitoring and evaluating progress.			X	X	X
	27	Formulating responses to threats and for an organisation as they arise,				X	X

187

PUBLIC RELATIONS INDUSTRY TRAINING GUIDE

		PUBLIC RELATIONS SKILLS Stage:	1	2	3	4	5
	28	Assessing the public relations implications of general management plans and decisions.				X	X
	29	Assessing the public relations implications for an organisation of the plans and decisions of other organisations, including: its market place; local and national government; the European community; national and international regulatory bodies; the media; special interest groups; the local community.			X X X X X X X	X X X X X X X	X X X X X X X
	30	Selecting external resources, such as photographers, designers, printers and researchers.			X	X	X
	31	Public speaking.			X	X	X
	32	Giving interviews					X
	33	Counselling and advisory technique.					X
	34	Risk and issue management.				X	X
	35	Crisis management.				X	X

BUSINESS SKILLS

				1	2	3	4	5
D	1	Communication:	Telephone technique	X	X	X	X	X
	2		Meeting technique	X	X	X	X	X
	3		Presentation technique		X	X	X	X
	4		Working as part of a team	X	X	X	X	X
	5		Working as part of an organisation	X	X	X	X	X
	6		Networking (clients, colleagues, contacts)		X	X	X	X
	7		Motivation and leadership			X	X	X
	8		Induction and orientation				X	X
	9		Interviewing and staff selection				X	X
	10	Organisational:	Work flow planning and setting priorities	X	X	X	X	X
	11		Time management		X	X	X	X
	12		Delegation and supervision		X	X	X	X
	13		Budget setting and control		X	X	X	X
	14		Team building and management				X	X
	15		Professional development of subordinates				X	X
	16		Design of financial controls					X
	17		Design of quality controls					X
	18	Analytical:	Analysing annual reports and financial data			X	X	X

Bibliography

Bell, Q, *The PR Business*, Kogan Page, 1991.

Bennis, W G, *Organisational Development: its Nature, Origins and Prospects*, Addison-Wesley, 1969.

Bernstein, D, *Company Image and Reality*, Holt, Rinehart & Winston, San Diego, Ca, 1984.

Biddlecombe, P (Ed), *Goodwill – the Wasted Asset*, Business Books, 1971.

Bowman, P and Ellis, N, *Manual of Public Relations*, Heinemman, 1984.

Bryan, P and Cronin, T, *Organisational Theory*, Mitchell Beazley, 1983.

Burke, W W, 'A comparison of management development and organisation development', *Management Science*, 1971.

Capper, A and Cunard, P, *The Public Relations Casebook*, Kogan Page, 1990.

Child, J, *Organisation – a Guide to Problems and Practice*, Harper & Row, 1984.

Coulson-Thomas, C, *Public Relations: A Practical Guide*, Macdonald and Evans, 1979.

Coulson-Thomas, C, *Public Relations is Your Business*, Business Books, 1981.

Cutlip, S, Center, A, and Broom, G, *Effective Public Relations*, Prentice-Hall, New Jersey, 1985.

de Bono, E, *The Use of Lateral Thinking*, Penguin, 1971.

Derriman, J, *Public Relations in Business Management*, University of London Press, 1964.

Douglas, T, *Complete Guide to Advertising*, Macmillan, 1985.

Doyle, P and Hart, N A, *Case Studies in International Marketing*, Heinemann, 1982.

Drew, J, *Doing Business in the European Community*, Butterworth, 1979.

Greenwood, W and Welsh, T (eds), *McNae's Essential Law for Journalists*, Butterworth, 1982.

Grunig, J and Hunt, T, *Managing Public Relations*, Holt, Rinehart & Winston, San Diego, Ca, 1983.

Handy, C B, *Understanding Organisations*, Penguin, 1976.

Harrison, R, 'When power conflicts trigger team spirit', *European Business*, Spring 1972.

Hart, N, *Industrial Marketing Communications*, Kogan Page, 1993.

Haywood, R, *All about PR*, McGraw-Hill, 1984.

Hermann, C F, 'Some consequences of crisis which limit the viability of organisations', *Administrative Science Quarterly*, June 1963, pp 61–82.

Hollis, *Press and Public Relations Annual*, 1986.

Howard, W (ed), *The Practice of Public Relations*, Heinemann 1982.

Jefkins, F, *Planned Press and Public Relations*, Blackie, 1986.

March, J G and Simon, H A, *Organisations*, Wiley, 1958.

Mendes, N, *This PR Consultancy Business*, Mendes, 1984.

Merrett, A J and Lehr, M E, *The Private Company Today: an Investigation into the Economic Position of the Unquoted Company in the United Kingdom*, Gower Press, 1971, p 25.

Moore, George S, *Managing Corporate Relations*, Gower Press, 1980.

Nally, M, *International Public Relations in Practice*, Kogan Page, 1991.

Newman, K, *Financial Marketing and Communications*, Holt, Rinehart & Winston, San Diego, 1984.

Oxley, H, *Principles of Public Relations*, Kogan Page, 1989.

Paliwoda, S J, *International Marketing*, Heinemann, 1986.

Peters, M, *In Search of Excellence*, Harper and Row, 1984.

Phillips, D, *Evaluating Press Coverage*, Kogan Page, 1992.

Piper, J, *The British Code of Sales Promotion Practice: Managing Sales Promotion*, Gower Press, 1980.

Porter, M E, *Cases in Competitive Strategy*, Collier Macmillan, 1983.

Ridgway, J, *Successful Media Relations: A Practioners' Guide*, Gower, 1984.

Samuels, J M and Smythe, D J, 'Profits, variability of profits and firm size', *Economica*, May 1968, pp 127–38.

Smith, G, *Local Government for Journalists*, LGC Communications, 1986.

Tunstall, J, *The Media in Britain*, Constable, 1983.

Watts, R, *Public Relations for Top Management*, Croner, 1977.

White, R, *Advertising: What it is and How to do it*, McGraw-Hill, New York, 1983.

Williams, J, *The Manual of Sales Promotion*, Innovation Ltd, 1983.

Wilmshurst, J, *The Fundamentals of Advertising*, Heinneman, 1985.

Wragg, D, *Targeting Media Relations*, Kogan Page, 1993.

Wragg, D, *Public Relations for Sales and Marketing Management*, Kogan Page, 1987.

Index